AVOIDING SEXUAL DANGERS

A Parent's Guide to Protecting Your Child

Julie C. Medlin, Ph.D. and Steven K. Knauts, Ph.D.

CONTENTS

Note to Reader:

Throughout this book we have included accounts of children, adolescents, and adults who we have worked with in our clinical practice. However, we have changed the names and other details in order to protect the confidentiality of the persons involved.

Chapter 1: Our Children Are Becoming Sexualized Too Early

Anyone looking at the boy in the waiting room would think he was a typical 5-year-old. Certainly his mother always believed that, until last month. He played video games, complained about school, and ate like a horse. He rode bikes with his friends and argued with his siblings. An average boy, his mother repeated to herself. A normal boy. Five weeks ago he was at home with his 3-year-old sister. Normally he couldn't stand his sister, but that day he seemed happy to play with her. The mother thought to herself, I should have known something was wrong. She remembered that day, hearing the two of them playing and running around the house. Then, hearing nothing. She went looking, and found them in his room. Found her little girl on the ground with her clothes off, with her little boy on top of her. As shocking as that discovery was, it paled next to what her daughter told her later - about how her brother put his private in her mouth. And then put it in her bottom. Now, as she and her son waited for the doctor, she hoped that someone would tell her what was going on. Why did he do it? And how did he ever get the idea to do this? How could this have happened?

The above story is fictional, but the details are drawn from thousands of cases we have seen in our practice. There used to be a time when we would have been shocked to hear that a 5-year-old child knew about oral and anal sex, much less engaged in these behaviors with his 3-year-old sister. Unfortunately, that time is long gone.

After having worked as psychologists with children for many years, we now routinely see children, including very young children, who are knowledgeable about adult sexual acts and are engaging in such acts on a regular basis.

However, most people are not aware of this disturbing trend in our culture – particularly regarding just how young the children can be.

Like the mother in the story, the parents we work with are stunned and shocked that their children have somehow developed advanced knowledge of sex and sexual behavior. The problem is being fueled by pornography, which is now readily accessible to children, thanks to the Internet and explosion of devices that provide easy access to the Internet such as smart phones and portable gaming devices.

We are seeing cases where apparently normal children, with no history of abuse or problems, are developing deviant sexual interests and behaviors after having viewed pornography online. For example, we recently saw a case where a teenage girl posted photos on the Internet of herself performing oral sex on a dog. This girl came from an apparently "normal" family with no history of abuse, and she had no history of emotional, behavioral or sexual problems. She said that she developed a sexual interest in animals after viewing such sites on the Internet.

We have also seen many cases of brothers who molested their younger sisters after viewing pornography on the Internet. The brothers wanted to try what they had seen so they turned to their younger sisters, as they had easy access to their sisters and figured their sisters wouldn't know what they were doing.

How Children Become Prematurely Sexualized

Many children in our culture are becoming prematurely sexualized because they are exposed to sexual material or sexual activity at too young of an age. As a result, the children can develop sexual interests and behaviors that are not normal for their age. Certainly, it is normal for children to have some exposure to sexual information and to do some sexual experimenting (see Chapter 2). But here we are referring to sexual experiences that can be damaging to children, as they are not developmentally appropriate.

There are three main ways that children can become prematurely sexualized:

Exposure to sexual material:

Children can become prematurely sexualized by being exposed to sexually suggestive or sexually explicit materials such as pornographic magazines, videos, or Internet images. Children may also be exposed to sexual material on TV shows or movies that are not considered pornographic but are sexually suggestive, such as soap operas, PG or R-rated movies, and music videos. There are also sexually suggestive cartoons that are shown on major TV networks such as Adult Swim on the Cartoon Network. We have seen many cases where children have acted out sexually after having seen such TV shows, and the parents had no idea that there were sexual themes in the cartoons their children were watching. There are also numerous types of pornographic cartoons on the Internet called *anime*, which are very graphic in their sexual depictions and sometimes involve scenes of sexual violence and bondage.

In the new Internet age, it can be very challenging for parents to protect their children from sexual materials, as they are now readily available on satellite, digital or cable TV and the Internet. We have seen numerous cases in our practice where a child has accessed pornography on the Internet at school or the public library, without the staff's knowledge. However, it seems to be more common that children are accessing pornography in their own homes or friends' or neighbors' homes, without their parents' knowledge.

For example, we saw a case of a 10-year-old boy who performed oral sex on his 3-year-old female cousin after his female neighbor showed him pornographic movies. The boy later explained that he was just doing what he saw in the movies. He did not realize that he had just committed sexual abuse. Unfortunately, we are seeing more and more cases like this where young children are being exposed to pornography and are acting out the sexual behaviors they have seen.

Exposure to sexual activity:

Just as children can become sexualized from seeing pornography, they can become sexualized from seeing sexual activity in person. We have seen many cases where children saw their parents having sex. In some cases, the parents forgot to lock their bedroom doors or left their doors open, assuming the children were asleep. However, the children ended up being awake and secretly watched their parents' sexual activity, often without the parents ever knowing. Unfortunately, there are some parents who know their children see their sexual activity, but they figure that the children need to learn about sex at some point.

Whether accidental or intentional, exposure to sexual activity can be very negative for children, especially young children. Children who have seen sexual activity often feel confused about what they have seen. They may think that the man is harming the woman. They may also be curious about what they have seen and want to try it with another child. We have seen many such children who have gotten on top of their siblings or younger children and tried to hump them, imitating the motions they saw. These children may view the sexual activity as a secretive, exciting, adult activity they want to try. They may view it as even more appealing when the parent tells them it is not for children.

Sexual Abuse:

Children can also become prematurely sexualized by being sexually abused. Most people think that child molesters are adult strangers lurking in the dark, waiting to kidnap our children. While there are some cases like that, especially highlighted in the media, that is not the typical child molester. Instead, child molesters are usually someone we know, who has ongoing contact with the child. They are friends, neighbors, and relatives. It is important to understand this in order to keep your child safe from abuse.

It is also important to know that about 20% of individuals arrested for sex offenses are under the age of 18[1]. So, it is not enough to just worry about adults who might molest your child. You also need to consider all of the children and teens who could pose a risk to your child. Just think of all of the children your child interacts with at school, on the playground, on the school bus, at church, parks, daycare, summer camp, and numerous other environments. Unfortunately, we have seen hundreds of children who have been sexually abused by older children in these places, as well as other places that were thought to be safe. Some of this abuse has even occurred during class or while adults were in the room. Consider the case of Tom who we saw in our clinic:

Tom is a 12-year-old boy who attended an exclusive private school. During the school's chess club, he fondled and penetrated a 7-year-old girl's vagina with his fingers while she sat on his lap. Tom was able to hide his behavior, as he fondled the girl while they were pulled up to a desk. None of the teachers or students in the room noticed that this was occurring, and the 7-year-old girl remained silent, as Tom had successfully "groomed" her so she would not tell. This sexual abuse went on for several months until the girl accidentally disclosed the abuse one day. The girl's parents were shocked and horrified when they learned that their daughter had been sexually abused by another child at her exclusive private school, and that the abuse had occurred in a classroom filled with children and teachers.

In another case, a 5-year-old girl was sexually abused by a 10-year-old boy in a play tube on the playground of a popular fast-food chain. Most parents would never think that their child could be molested in an indoor playground just a few feet away from them. However, those play tubes provide the perfect opportunity for sexually aggressive children to molest other children, as the play tubes are often opaque and high above the ground.

In yet another case, an 8-year-old boy was anally raped by a 9-year-old male classmate in the bathroom at school. The 9-year-old threatened to kill him if he told anyone. After the abuse, the 8-year-old began losing control of his bowels, defecating on himself at home and school. His parents had no idea why he was suddenly having this problem. He then ended up molesting two 6-year-old boys in his neighborhood. The 6-year-old boys told about the abuse, and the 8-year-old then told about his own victimization by the 9-year-old. Unfortunately, cases such as these are becoming more and more common. In fact, we routinely see such cases in our counseling center.

What Happens When Children Become Prematurely Sexualized

Children who are prematurely sexualized may engage in inappropriate or abusive sexual behaviors. The worst case scenario, as noted above, is that the child may molest other children and may grow up to become an adult sex offender. Fortunately, research suggests that most sexually abused children do not end up molesting other children. It is more likely that the child may show lower-level sexualized behaviors such as frequent masturbation or making sexual comments to others. This can result in social alienation, as the child's peers may no longer want to play with the child due to the sexualized behaviors. The child may also miss out on play dates as the parents of other children no longer feel comfortable allowing their child to socialize with the sexualized child.

Sexualized behavior can also result in the child being kicked out of daycare or school. In fact, we have seen many cases of children brought in by their parents who are distraught that their child has been kicked out of school due to inappropriate sexual behaviors. Premature sexualization can also result in the child becoming preoccupied with sexual thoughts at the expense of other activities. For example, the child may become so focused on masturbation that he or she has difficulty concentrating in class. The child may also become obsessed with trying to access pornography, and may sacrifice sleep in order to get up in the middle of the night to view Internet pornography while the parents are asleep.

In addition to sexual acting out, children who have been prematurely sexualized – particularly those who have been sexually abused – may develop emotional or behavioral problems. For example, the child can develop emotional problems such as:

- nightmares
- anxiety
- depression

- difficulty paying attention
- wetting the bed
- flashbacks of the abuse

Or the child can develop behavioral problems such as:

- fighting
- running away
- throwing tantrums
- lying

- setting fires
- stealing
- using drugs or alcohol
- skipping school
- smearing feces

These problems can result not just from sexual abuse by an adult, but also from sexual abuse by an older child. In fact, sexual abuse committed by children may actually cause more emotional damage to the victims than abuse committed by adults. One reason for this is the victims often do not recognize that the sexual activity was abuse since the perpetrator was a child or teen. This can result in the victim not telling anyone about the abuse, which then prevents the victim from being able to receive counseling to heal from the abuse. Victims may also worry that they will get in trouble if they tell. Unfortunately, many children do not understand that only the older children should get in trouble for the sexual activity.

In our experience, when most children are asked what would happen if a 12-year-old child did sexual touching with a 6-year-old, they think that both children would get in trouble. Sadly, we have also found that many parents share this belief. It should be that only the older child is held responsible, as the 6-year-old is not capable of consenting to sexual activity with a 12-year-old. A child that young cannot consent because of their young age, as well as because of the significant power difference between a 12-year-old and 6-year-old. The 12-year-old would have a significant power advantage over the 6-year-old based on their physical size, knowledge, and emotional maturity.

Sexual abuse committed by children can also be especially damaging because the victim may think that the sexual abuse is a cool, secretive behavior that they should engage in with other children. They may then act out these sexually abusive behaviors with other children.

Protecting Children

How, then, do we keep our children from being

prematurely sexualized? Unfortunately, it is not enough to install parental controls on our computers and TVs at home. What about the TVs and computers at their friends' houses? What about the computers at the school? What about the cell phones of other students, cell phones that can easily connect to pornographic websites? What about the PSPs that kids use to play videogames that can access porn as well? Even if we could control all of these electronic devices that are proliferating all around us, we are still left with the potential problem of other children being exposed to porn on these devices, and then interacting with our children. And children who have been exposed to porn often want to share their new discoveries with other children and may even want to try the sexual behaviors.

Unfortunately, once a child is exposed to the graphic images in porn, there is no way to erase this from the child's memory. It then becomes a matter of helping the child process what he or she has seen and hoping the child will not continue to think about those images, act out the behaviors from the images, or seek out more porn.

In the case of exposure to pornography and adult sexual activity, the key is to recognize when and where the child has potential access, and then to prevent that access. This book provides practical suggestions for both recognizing and stopping such access. With respect to sexual abuse, the key is of course to prevent your child from having contact with sexual abusers. This is not simply a case of advising the child of "stranger danger," because the great majority of sexual offenses are perpetrated by someone the child knows. Unfortunately, this makes your job as a parent much more difficult because it means you have to figure out who you can reasonably trust. This is not an easy task since sexual abusers, whether they are adults or children, do not look any different than non-abusers. This book also offers tips on how you can protect your children by having an open and honest relationship with them, giving them guidance regarding potential sexual abuse, and avoiding potential high-risk situations.

While the task of protecting children from sexual abuse and exposure to sexual material can seem daunting, we believe that education and knowledge is the parents' best defense. It is our hope that parents who read this book will come away with the tools they need to protect their children, and to properly intervene in those cases where their child has been prematurely sexualized.

---

[1] Snyder, H.N. (2000). *Sexual assault of young children as reported to law enforcement: Victim, incident, and offender characteristics.* Washington, D.C.: U.S. Department of Justice, Office of Justice Programs, Bureau of Justice Statistics.

Chapter 2: Sexual Behavior in Children

Introduction

As parents, we are often in the role of trying to understand our child's behavior and trying to figure out if the behavior is normal. We wonder if other children are doing the same thing as our child, and wonder if the latest behavior is just a "phase" they will grow out of. For example, parents of toddlers often wonder if their child's tantrums are signs of a serious behavior problem, or if their child's sudden change in sleep habits is something to worry about. However, most parents are able to find their way through the developmental thicket, either by talking to other parents or their child's pediatrician, reading parenting books, or just waiting to see if the phase passes. This approach usually works for the various developmental issues that parents face as their children grow up. However, there is one area where there seems to be a lot of confusion and often poor advice, even from medical and mental health professionals. That area is sexual behavior in children.

It is often unclear to parents whether or not it is normal for children to show sexual behavior, and if so, what sexual behaviors are normal at what age. For example is it normal for:

- 5-year-old Joey to be pulling down his pants in the bathroom at school, showing his penis to the other boys?
- 8-year-old Sarah to playfully touch her 4-year-old sister's vagina when they take a bath together?

- 14-year-old Antonio to sexually experiment with his 11-year-old cousin? Would it make any difference if that cousin were male or female?

It has always been difficult for parents to know what sexual behaviors to expect in their children, as this subject has traditionally been taboo in our culture. Fortunately, there has been much more open discussion about these issues in recent years; however, the parents' job has gotten more and more complicated as new technology has allowed for a much wider range of sexual experiences in children. As we discussed in Chapter 1, children are much more able to access porn now than in the past, as Internet access is readily available. Children are also now able to send sexual text messages, called "sexting," a behavior that was not possible in the past. They are also able to send nude pictures of themselves and others over the Internet with ease. With social networking sites like Facebook, children are now able to meet strangers with whom they can arrange to meet and engage in sexual activity. All of this has forced parents to deal with an increasingly complicated sexual landscape. For example, parents are faced with new questions such as:

- Is it normal for their teenager to send sexual texts or share pornographic images via their cell phone?

- What about 15-year-old Max who has been viewing Internet pornography after his parents go to sleep at night? Is this just the typical behavior of a curious teenage boy who is trying to learn about sex?

- What about 16-year-old Samantha who has her age listed as 21 on her Facebook page and has chatted with several adult males about their sexual interests?

Most parents, and even professionals, have difficulty answering these questions and knowing what to do if their child were to show such behaviors. This chapter will provide parents with guidelines about how to evaluate their children's behaviors and how to determine if the behaviors should warrant concern and intervention.

Is It "Normal" for Children to Show Sexual Behavior?

Yes. In fact, most adults report that they engaged in some sexual behavior when they were children. Over 84% of male and female college students reported having had sexual experiences with peers before starting high school.[1] As you might expect, younger children are less likely to engage in sexual behavior than older children. Only about 15% of women and 24% of men reported that they had sexual experiences before they entered elementary school. Many more women and men reported having had sexual experiences once they were in elementary school, with 58% of the women and 63% of the men reporting such sexual experiences. These percentages stayed about the same for junior high, although the frequency and type of sexual acts may have changed.

These numbers show that many children do engage in sexual behaviors. However, not all sexual behavior is the same. For example, there is a big difference between a 5-year-old kissing a classmate on the cheek, and a 5-year-old "kissing" the classmate on the vagina. The first would be considered normal while the second would not. The question then becomes when is sexual behavior considered normal versus abnormal? In our clinical experience, parents and even mental health professionals are often unsure where to draw the line.

What is "Normal" Sexual Play?

In a nutshell, sexual play among children is considered to be normal when it is between non-related children of roughly the same age, is consensual, and only involves sexual behaviors that are appropriate for a child's age. Let's look at each of these criteria:

1) **Non-Related:** The children should not be from the same family. It is considered abnormal for close relatives, such as siblings, to engage in sexual activity with each other. This extends to children who are living together as relatives, but may not be biologically related, such as stepsiblings.

2) **Age:** The general rule of thumb is that children who are engaging in sexual activity with each other should be no more than 2 years apart in age. The reason for this is that there is a big developmental difference between children who are 3 or more years apart in age. For example, consider the emotional and physical size differences between a 3-year-old and 6-year-old. The 3-year-old is likely to be much smaller and less verbally, intellectually, and emotionally developed than a 6-year-old. The 3-year-old is also able to be easily manipulated by the older child, as younger children typically look up to older children and want to please them.

We have seen many cases where older children have been able to trick or manipulate younger children into sexual acts, as the younger child was not even aware of the sexual nature of the behavior. For example, an older child may trick a young child into licking his penis by telling the young child it tastes like a lollipop.

In general, age differences are much more significant among younger children than among older children. For example, there is not as much difference in power and emotional development between a 17-year-old and 14-year-old as there is between a 12-year-old and 9-year-old. In the first case, the two teens have both likely experienced puberty while in the second case, the 12-year-old may have while the 9-year-old has not. Therefore, when trying to assess the power difference between two children, it is important to consider the developmental stages of each child.

3) **Consent:** Sexual play is considered to be consensual when both children agree to the sexual play, they understand what they are doing, and there is no significant power difference between the children. In order for the children to truly agree to the sexual play, there must be no bribes, threats, force, manipulation, or intimidation involved. Here are some examples of tactics children use to pressure others into sexual activity:

Bribe:	"If you touch my wee wee, then I'll let you play with my videogame."
Threat:	"If you tell, I'll say you started it."
Force:	Pinning down the other child
Manipulation:	"It's a fun game. All the kids are playing it.
Intimidation:	"You better do it or I'll beat you up."

In order for sexual activity to be consensual, the children involved must understand what they are doing, meaning they should not be tricked into engaging in sexual behavior.

Older children sometimes trick younger children into sexual activity by presenting it as a game such as "doctor" or touching the younger child during "wrestling." If there is any deception involved, then the sexual activity is not consensual.

There should also be no significant power differences between the children. As we discussed earlier, there can be a power difference between the children if one child is significantly older than the other. However, there are many other ways in which there can be a power difference, such as a difference in the children's physical size. A much larger child can intimidate or force a smaller child into unwanted sexual activity. There can also be a power difference if there is a big intellectual difference between the children, as in the case of a mentally retarded child who is involved with a child of average IQ. A difference in social status could also result in a power difference, such as if one child is popular while the other is not. The popular child may be able to pressure the other child into sexual activity, especially if the less popular child wants to be liked and accepted. This dynamic could also occur between children where one is always the leader and the other is always the follower.

A power difference can also occur when there is a big difference in sexual knowledge between children. For example, a child who has been sexually abused and/or exposed to pornography usually knows much more about sexual matters than a child who has not. We have seen many cases like this where a child who has been sexually abused or exposed to pornography has then introduced other children to sexual information, materials, or behaviors.

4) **Developmentally Appropriate:** As we discussed earlier, there are "normal" sexual behaviors among children. However, the type of sexual behavior that is considered normal depends upon the child's age. The general rule of thumb is that any type of sexual penetration (oral, vaginal, or anal) is considered atypical or abnormal in children who are under age 10. So if an 8-year-old is engaging in oral sex, then we would consider that behavior to be abnormal. We would also consider it to be a "red flag" that suggests the child may have been sexually abused or exposed to pornography or adult sexual activity. Later in this chapter, we will discuss the specific sexual behaviors that are "red flags" at given ages.

Is My Child's Sexual Behavior Normal?

Check if your child's sexual behavior involves any of the following:

☐ Includes oral, vaginal, or anal penetration before age 10
☐ Involves physical harm to my child or anyone else
☐ Violates others' personal boundaries
☐ Violates rules at school, home or other setting
☐ Causes problems at home or school
☐ Results in your child being disciplined at school
☐ Involves another person who does not agree to the sexual activity
☐ Involves another child who is 3 or more years younger
☐ Involves force, bribes, or manipulation of someone else
☐ Is against the law
☐ Interferes with your child's development or functioning

If you checked any of these then your child's sexual behavior may not be normal.

Typical Sexual Behavior at Different Ages

Ages 0 to 5:

Fetuses can show erections and vaginal lubrication while still in the uterus. Thus, genitals can show a reaction to stimulation even before birth. After birth, babies and infants explore their bodies just as they explore the world around them. In their exploration, they usually discover that it feels good when their genitals are touched or rubbed. They may then touch their genitals during diaper changes or baths. Whether or not they continue to openly engage in this behavior will depend on how their parent or caretaker responds. If the parent punishes or admonishes the child, then the child may stop engaging in the behavior, at least in front of the parent.

Many parents report that their young children fondle themselves. Approximately 60% of parents reported that their sons in the age range of 2 to 5 touched their own genitals at home.[2] And, approximately 44% of parents reported this same behavior in their daughters ages 2 to 5. Thus, it is common for young children to touch their own genitals at home. It is less common for children to touch their genitals in public. About 27% of parents reported that their boys, ages 2 to 5, did this while only 15% of parents reported this behavior in their daughters.

While young children may touch and rub their genitals, they are not usually doing it to achieve orgasm, as a teen or adult would masturbate to orgasm. By the age of 4 or 5, most children learn that it is not socially acceptable to engage in sexual behaviors in front of others.

During toilet training, children become focused on bathroom activities, which may include wanting to watch others use the toilet. By age 4, children may show their genitals to others, and want to see others' genitals. 27% of parents reported that their sons and daughters (ages 2 to 5) tried to see other people when they were nude. Fewer children (approximately 16% of boys and 14% of girls ages 2 to 5) showed their genitals to adults. Many children in this age range (43% of boys and 44% of girls) try to touch their mother's or other women's breasts.

Children in this age group may want to play "house" in which they act out the mother doll and father doll kissing and lying in bed together. They are repeating what they have seen and heard, and are acting out gender roles. However, most young children do not have any knowledge of adult sexual behaviors.[3] If they are aware of such behaviors, then this is a red flag of possible sexual abuse or exposure to sexual activity or pornography. In addition to playing "house," children in this age group may play "doctor," repeating what they have experienced at the doctor's office by pretending to be the doctor to a doll or other child.

Some children in this age range touch other children on their genitals. However, this behavior is not very common, with only 5% of boys and 9% of girls engaging in this behavior. This behavior, like many other sexual behaviors, is much more common among children who have been sexually abused.

"Red Flags" for Possible Sexual Abuse

We consider a sexual behavior to be a red flag when it:
- occurs more frequently than expected
- is developmentally inappropriate
- is more common among sexually abused children

Frequency is important as it reflects whether or not a child is preoccupied or obsessed with a sexual behavior. For example, if a 4-year-old touches her vagina only a few times a day, while in the bath or when on the toilet, then this would be considered normal behavior. However, if that same child touched her vagina so many times a day that her vagina became red and irritated then we would consider that a "red flag." We also consider developmentally inappropriate sexual behaviors such as oral sex to be a "red flag" in a young child.

When trying to determine if a sexual behavior is a "red flag," we also look to see if that specific sexual behavior is much more common among sexually abused children. For example, sexually abused children are much more likely than non-abused children to talk about sexual acts and to ask others to engage in sexual acts with them. In fact, based on ratings of parents, talking about sexual acts is at least 8 times more common among sexually abused preschool aged children than among non-abused children of the same age. And, asking others to engage in sexual acts is 30 to 40 times more common among preschool aged children who were sexually abused.

The following is a list of sexualized behaviors that are much more common among preschool aged sexually abused boys and girls than among non-abused children. We use the term "sexualized" because not all of these behaviors are clearly sexual in nature. In fact, these behaviors can be fairly subtle and many people probably would not know that these behaviors are associated with a history of sexual abuse. This list, and the lists that follow, are drawn from research conducted for the Child Sexual Behavior Inventory[4]:

Red Flags for **CHILDREN** Ages 2 to 5

- Touching another child's private parts
- Trying to have sexual intercourse with another child or adult
- Putting mouth on another child or adult's sex parts
- Asking others to engage in sexual acts
- Showing private parts to adults
- Being overly friendly with males they don't know well
- Talking flirtatiously
- Talking about sexual acts
- Trying to put tongue in other person's mouth when kissing
- Hugging adults they do not know well
- Being very interested in the opposite sex
- Knowing more about sex than other children their age

The sexualized behaviors listed above were reported significantly more by parents of sexually abused children than by parents of children who had not been sexually abused. You can use this list as a quick reference to determine if your child is displaying sexual behaviors that could be a sign of possible sexual abuse.

Keep in mind that some non-abused children may display some of these sexual behaviors. Therefore, showing some of these sexual behaviors does not necessarily mean that a child has been sexually abused. The more of these sexual behaviors a child displays, and the greater the frequency of these behaviors, the greater the likelihood that the child has been sexually abused or at least exposed to inappropriate sexual situations or material.

In addition to the list above, there are other sexual behaviors that are "red flags" just for girls while there are other behaviors that are "red flags" just for boys.

Below is a list of other sexualized behaviors that are more common among sexually abused preschool aged girls than non-abused girls:

Red Flags for **GIRLS** Ages 2 to 5

- Masturbating with her hand
- Touching her private parts when in public places
- Touching an adult's private parts
- Making sexual sounds (sighs, moans, heavy breathing)
- Rubbing her body against people or furniture
- Putting objects in her vagina or rectum
- Pretending that dolls or stuffed animals are having sex
- Kissing adults she does not know well
- Getting upset when adults are kissing or hugging

Below is a list of other sexualized behaviors that are more common among sexually abused preschool aged *boys* than among non-abused boys:

Red Flags for **BOYS** Ages 2 to 5

- Talking about wanting to be the opposite sex
- Drawing sex parts when drawing pictures of people
- Masturbating with a toy or object (blanket, pillow, etc)
- Trying to look at pictures of nude or partially dressed people
- Kissing other children he does not know well
- Wanting to watch TV or movies that show nudity or sex
- Trying to undress adults against their will (opening pants, shirt, etc.)

If your child shows many of these "red flag" sexual behaviors, then we recommend that you take your child to see a mental health professional who specializes in evaluating sexual behaviors in children. The mental health professional can then gather more information from you and your child in order to assess if your child may have a sexual problem and/or been sexually traumatized in some way.

Ages 6 to 9:

Children in this age range seem to display fewer sexual behaviors than younger children, or at least fewer parents are reporting these sexual behaviors. For example, fewer parents report that their children at this age are touching their genitals at home or in public. This may be due to the children learning that it is not socially acceptable to touch their genitals in front of others. However, a significant percentage of parents still report this behavior. Specifically, 40% of parents reported that their sons touched their genitals at home and 21% of parents reported that their girls did the same. It also appears that children at this age are much less likely than young children to touch their mother's or other women's breasts. Only 14% of boys and 16% of girls in this age range engage in this behavior.

Children in this age range may find other ways to stimulate their genitals. For example, young girls may discover that it feels good to let running water from the tub faucet hit their vaginas while boys may discover that climbing up a pole feels good on their penises. Children in this age range may begin to show a desire for privacy. For example, they may put a towel around their nude bodies after a bath or ask that others knock on their bathroom or bedroom door before entering.

Children in this age range often tell dirty jokes, although they may not fully understand the meaning of the jokes. They may also ask questions such as "Where did I come from?" and may giggle when people kiss. They may show mixed feelings about seeing kissing and sexual behaviors, alternating between being repulsed and being curious. Children in this age range usually have more opportunities for sexual behaviors with other children, given that they attend school and have more access to peers. Some of them may hold hands and kiss other children, pretending that they are dating. They are most likely repeating what they have seen. About 8% of boys, but only 1% of girls in this age range touch other children on their genitals.

The following is a list of sexualized behaviors that are much more common among sexually abused boys and girls ages 6 to 9 than among non-abused children:

Red Flags for **CHILDREN** Ages 6 to 9

- Stands too close to people
- Masturbates with hand
- Touches another child's private parts
- Tries to have sexual intercourse with other child or adult
- Rubs body against people or furniture
- Pretends that dolls or stuffed animals are having sex
- Overly friendly with men they don't know well
- Kisses other children they don't know well
- Talks flirtatiously
- Tries to undress other children against their will (opening pants, shirt, etc.)
- Is very interested in the opposite sex
- Knows more about sex than other children their age

Here are the lists of other sexualized behaviors that are much more common in sexually abused children of each sex:

Red Flags for **GIRLS** Ages 6 to 9

- Touching or trying to touch their mother's or other women's breasts
- Masturbating with toy or object (blanket, pillow, toy)
- Hugging adults they do not know well

Red Flags for **BOYS** Ages 6 to 9

- Drawing sex parts when drawing pictures of people
- Putting mouth on another child or adult's private parts
- Touching animal's private parts
- Asking others to engage in sexual acts with him
- Talking about sexual acts
- Getting upset when adults are kissing or hugging
- Showing private parts to children

Ages 10 to 12:

Children at this age tend to focus on relationships with peers. Some engage in kissing and fondling with peers. Some engage in sexual activities with children of the same sex; however, most experiences are with the opposite sex. It is relatively rare for children under age 13 to engage in oral, anal, or vaginal sex. When adults were asked about their childhoods, only 9% of females and 16% of males reported having engaged in oral sex before high school. Anal sex was even less common, with only 3% of females and 4% of males having engaged in this behavior in childhood.

As for vaginal sex, only 3.1% of girls and 8.4% of boys reported that they had vaginal intercourse before age 13[5]. Vaginal insertion (with an object or finger) is more common, with 18% of females and 22% of males having engaged in this behavior[6].

The following is the list of sexualized behaviors that are much more common among sexually abused children ages 10 to 12 than among non-abused children:

Red Flags for **CHILDREN** Ages 10 to 12

- Talks about sexual acts
- Overly friendly with men they don't know well
- Kisses other children they don't know well
- Talks flirtatiously
- Hugs adults they do not know well
- Knows more about sex than other children their age

The following is the list of other sexualized behaviors that are much more common among sexually abused girls in this age range, followed by the corresponding list for boys:

Red Flags for **GIRLS** Ages 10 to 12

- Drawing sex parts when drawing pictures of people
- Making sexual sounds
- Kissing adults they do not know well
- Wanting to watch TV or movies that show nudity or sex

Red Flags for **BOYS** Ages 10 to 12

- Stands too close to people
- Touches private parts when in public places
- Touches or tries to touch women's breasts
- Touches another child's private parts
- Touches private parts when at home
- Rubs body against people or furniture
- Tries to look at people when they are nude or undressing

Ages 13 to 17

Teens may engage in a wide range of sexual behaviors such as fondling, oral sex, and vaginal intercourse. The most common sexual behavior is masturbation, with about 68% of boys and 43% of girls, ages 14 to 17, reporting that they have masturbated within the past year[7]. Most teens do not engage in other sexual activities before age 14, but they are much more likely to engage in vaginal intercourse as they get older.[8] Among teens ages 14 to 15, only 9.9% of boys and 12.4% of girls reported having had vaginal intercourse. However, among teens ages 16 to 17, 30.3% of boys and 31.6% of girls reported having had vaginal intercourse.[9]

The average age of first sexual intercourse (sex) is about 16 ½ years old for males and females.[10] According to a 2009 study, 46% of U.S. high schoolers (9th to 12th grades) reported that they had had sexual intercourse[11], with the percentages for boys and girls being roughly the same. It appears that most teens do not engage in sexual intercourse on a regular basis. For example, 40% of 17-year-old boys reported having had sex within the past year, but only 27% reported having had sex within the past 90 days[12].

As you might expect, teenage girls are much more likely than boys to have only one sexual partner. 30% of girls said they had just one sexual partner, versus only about 10% of the boys[13].

> *What is the average age that teens lose their virginity?*
> *16 ½*

Among teens who reported having sexual intercourse, 80% of boys and 69% of girls indicated that they used a condom during their last sexual experience. While on the one hand it is encouraging that so many teens are at least trying to practice safe sex, it is also disturbing that so many – a fifth of all males, and nearly a third of all females surveyed – did *not*.

What about oral sex? Many teens do not view oral sex as being as "big of a deal" as sexual intercourse.[14] Given this, some teens will engage in oral sex, while waiting to have vaginal intercourse. In one study, at ages 15 to 17, about 13% of boys and 11% of girls had engaged in heterosexual oral sex, but not vaginal intercourse[15]. However, most teens under 18 have not engaged in oral or anal sex.

As you might expect, people who engaged in sexual activity *before* high school were more likely to have sexual intercourse at an earlier age. Also, people who had sexual experiences before age 12 engaged in more extensive sexual activity, and at earlier ages, when they were teens[16].

How many teens report engaging in sexual activity with the same sex? Not many. Only 5 to 7% of teens, ages 15 to 19, reported having such contact[17].

Have sexual behaviors changed over the past 50 years?

Yes. Research suggests there has been a big increase in sexual behaviors in childhood over time. Of adults surveyed in 1998, 87.2% of the males reported having engaged in some sexual behavior before high school while only 68% of males in 1948 reported such. The difference for the females is much more significant, with 84.4% of those in 1998 reporting childhood sexual experiences compared to only 42% of those in 1948. Also, there was a four-fold increase in the percentage of females who had engaged in sexual intercourse by college.

More recent research suggests that since 1992, more men and women report that they have engaged in oral sex and anal sex[18]. Thus, it appears that people may be engaging in a broader range of sexual behaviors than in the past. This may be due to people having more exposure to pornography which tends to depict many different sexual acts.

When does sexual behavior become a problem?

Earlier in this chapter we described the criteria for "normal" sexual behavior in children. Using these same criteria, sexual behavior in children is considered abnormal or problematic when there is a 3 or more year age difference between the children, the sexual activity occurs between close biological relatives, and/or the sexual activity is not consensual. However, there are many other sexual behaviors in children that may not fall in these categories, but that could be considered problematic, such as sexual behaviors[19] that:

- Put the child at risk of being harmed by others
- Disrupt with the child's daily functioning
- Interfere with the child's relationships
- Cause physical harm to the child's body
- Violate rules at school or elsewhere

Behaviors that put the child at risk:

Some sexual behaviors are problematic because they put the child at risk of being harmed in some way. For example, 13-year-old Shameka sneaks out of her house at night to meet men in their twenties for sex. Her behavior is putting her at risk for being sexually assaulted and contracting an STD. We have seen many cases in our clinical practice where teenage girls, particularly those with a prior history of sexual abuse, view promiscuity as a way to rebel against their parents and to feel "cool" and accepted by males. Now with the easy accessibility to the Internet, girls can rebel from their own bedrooms by meeting older males online. They can even make money by posting nude photos of themselves or engaging in sexual acts via their webcam. Unfortunately, there are many sexual predators online who are looking for vulnerable girls and who go to great lengths to lure the teen into sexual activity, playing to the teen's insecurity, rebelliousness, and desire for attention.

Behaviors that cause problems in the child's daily functioning:

Some sexual behaviors are problematic because they interfere with the child's functioning on a day-to-day basis. For example, 15-year-old John has difficulty concentrating and staying awake in class because he is losing hours of sleep each night so he can secretly view pornography on the Internet while his parents are asleep. Clearly, John's sexual behavior is interfering with his daily functioning in school. John may also be developing an addiction to pornography if he has difficulty stopping the destructive sexual behavior and continues to engage in the behavior despite the negative consequences.

In our practice, we are seeing an increasing number of teens being brought in by their concerned parents, as the teens have become addicted to Internet pornography and go to great lengths to obtain it despite preventive measures taken by their parents. These teens' social and family relationships often suffer as well, as the teens withdraw from social interactions in order to spend more time on the computer or in hiding their behavior.

Behaviors that cause problems in the child's relationships:

Some sexual behaviors are problematic because they interfere with the child's relationships with others. For example, 7-year-old Sarah often makes sexual comments to her classmates and constantly puts her hands down her pants in class to touch herself. She has few friends, as her classmates think her behaviors are weird and gross. Also consider the case of 16-year-old Brittany who has been ostracized by her female peers because she gives "head" to random boys in the bathroom. In this case, Brittany is engaging in a consensual sexual act with peers, but she is doing it in an inappropriate place and in an indiscriminate way. As a result, her friendships suffer, not to mention her own self-respect and self-worth.

Behaviors that cause harm to the child's body:

Some children's sexual behavior is problematic because it results in harm to their bodies. For example, 8-year-old Megan masturbates many times a day, to the point that her vagina is red and swollen, and she repeatedly contracts yeast infections. We often see this type of behavior in young children who have been sexually abused and who have difficulty inhibiting their impulses. However, we have also seen cases of older children and adults who intentionally harm themselves as part of their sexual activity.

For example, we have seen men who puncture their penises with needles, as they are sexually aroused to pain. We also had a case of a teenage girl who penetrated herself with a toilet plunger, to the point that her vagina bled profusely. Clearly, these sexual behaviors are problematic and warrant professional intervention.

Behaviors that violate rules:

Sexual behaviors can be problematic if they violate rules such as at school, summer camp, daycare, etc. Sexual behavior in school is considered problematic because it violates the school rules and can interfere with the students feeling safe and being able to focus on their work. Examples include teens making out in the hallways and engaging in sexual activity in the bathrooms, under the bleachers, and on the ball field. These sexual behaviors become even more problematic when they are nonconsensual, such as boys grabbing girls' breasts and buttocks as they pass by in the hallway. We are seeing an increasing number of these sexual harassment cases, as the school environment becomes more sexually charged over time. We are also seeing many cases of students sharing pornography with their classmates via their cell phones and PSPs, as well as accessing pornography on the school computers despite blocking measures. In addition, students are easily sending sexual text messages to other students during class via their cell phones, as they no longer have to worry about the risk of getting caught handing a note to a classmate.

Range of Sexual Behaviors in Children

We have been talking about normal versus abnormal sexual behaviors in children. However, there are many shades of gray between these categories. In fact, we can conceptualize sexual behavior as falling along a continuum, with "normal" sexual behavior at one end and sexual abuse at the other end:

Based on this continuum, children can be categorized into four groups[20]:

Normal Sexual Exploration: GROUP 1

This category involves sexual play that is considered to be normal or within expected behaviors for children at their age. The sexual play involves:

- Consensual sexual contact
- Children of similar age and size
- Friends rather than siblings

Abby is 6 years old and in the 1st grade. She refers to Derek, another first grader, as her boyfriend. Abby pretends to be a princess while Derek pretends to her prince. They kiss each other on the lips and hold hands. Both children agree to the kissing and holding hands, and neither child has a history of sexual abuse or exposure to pornography. Abby and Derek's behavior would be considered normal sexual exploration.

Sexually Reactive: GROUP 2

Children in this group display more advanced or frequent sexual behaviors than the children in Group 1. However, their sexual behaviors do not include sexual activity with others. Instead, their sexual behaviors usually involve masturbation and/or sexual comments. These children:

- Have sexual knowledge beyond what is appropriate for their age
- May feel shame, guilt, and anxiety about sexuality
- Have often been sexually abused or exposed to pornography

John is 8 years old and he often has his hands down the front of his pants so he can touch his penis. His parents have to frequently ask him to stop touching himself. He makes humping motions on his bed and the sofa. He often talks about girls on TV who look "hot" and he says he wants to "do" them. John has seen his older brother's Playboy magazines and has seen pornography on the Internet. John falls in Group 2 because his sexual knowledge is advanced for his age and he is preoccupied with sexual issues.

Extensive Mutual Sexual Behaviors: GROUP 3

Children in this group engage in the full spectrum of adult sexual behaviors such as sexual intercourse. They also show more frequent and extensive sexual behavior than the children in Group 2. These children:

- Tend to engage in sexual play with children their age rather than younger children
- Do not usually use force or coercion
- Tend to have a casual attitude about sex
- Often have been physically, emotionally, or sexually abused
- Use sex as way to relate to others

Jennifer is 10 years old and she is having sexual intercourse with her 11-year-old male neighbor. She has also had sex with several other boys her age, and she writes sexual notes to boys at school asking if they want to have sex. Jennifer was sexually abused by her stepfather at age 5 and she has shown sexualized behaviors since then. Jennifer does not understand why her mother and teachers are upset about her sexual behaviors. Jennifer falls in Group 3 because her sexual behaviors are advanced for her age, as most children her age are not having sexual intercourse.

Children Who Molest: GROUP 4

Children in this group molest other children, either by targeting much younger children or using coercion or bribes. These children:

- Engage in sex play that has an impulsive, compulsive, aggressive quality
- May associate sex with anger, loneliness, and fear
- Have little empathy for the children they molest
- Usually do not stop without specialized treatment

Devin is a 9-year-old boy who is in foster care. He was recently moved to a new foster home because in his last placement he tricked the foster mother's 3-year-old son into sucking his penis. Devin told the boy it was a game, and offered to play trucks with him if the boy did it. In his after-school program, Devin stuck his hand down the underwear of a 5-year-old girl, and told her he would beat her up if she told. Devin is a good example of a child who falls in Group 4.

What Can Parents Do To Promote Healthy Sexual Development in Their Children?

There are 4 steps parents can take to encourage healthy sexual development in their child:

1) Parents can model healthy boundaries and healthy intimate relationships. Children learn a lot from watching their parents and others around them. For example, if a child sees his father grabbing his mother's breast as she walks by, the child may believe that this is how males should treat females.

2) Parents can take steps to control the sexual messages their child is exposed to from outside sources such as TV and movies. For example, parents can install parental controls on their TVs, computers, and internet-accessible devices. See Chapter 7 for detailed information about how to protect your child from pornography.

3) Parents can take steps to minimize the child's risk of being molested. See Chapter 6 for detailed information about protecting your child from abusers.

4) Parents can teach their children about genitalia, puberty, and sex so that the child receives accurate information about this. This also allows the parent to communicate to their child their own beliefs and values about sex. In addition, such information can help protect the child against sexual abuse.

How and When Should Parents Talk To Their Children About Sexual Issues?

It is recommended that when children are between the ages of 2 to 5, parents teach their child the correct terms for genitalia and the difference between appropriate versus inappropriate touching. This is important because it makes it more likely that your child will recognize if someone tries to molest them. It also makes it more likely that your child will respond assertively in that situation, and will tell you about it. There are books written specifically to help parents talk to their children about what constitutes sexual abuse. For a list of those books, see Chapter 6. For children ages 8 to 12, it is recommended that their parents talk to them about puberty so the children know what to expect as their bodies begin to change.

So, when should you talk to your child about sex? We believe that this depends on several factors such as when the child is developmentally ready to learn about it, which is usually by age 10. The timing also depends on when your child is likely to learn about sex from other sources, such as from their older siblings, peers, or from TV shows. This will vary from family to family, and will depend on the child's home environment, neighborhood, school, and the parents' style of parenting. We recommend that parents be the *first* ones to talk to their children about sex, so parents need to have this talk with their child as soon as they think their child may learn about sex from another source. For many families, this means talking to your child about sex sooner rather than later. However, children who live in very protected environments may not need to know about sex until age 9 or 10.

Consider the case of 10-year-old Susan. Susan's mother home-schools her and her siblings, and Susan and her siblings do not watch TV, except for pre-recorded educational programs that are screened carefully by her parents. There are parental controls on all computers to which Susan and her siblings have access, and Susan and her siblings socialize only with other home-schooled children whose parents have the same restrictions in their home. Susan's mother has chosen to wait until Susan is 10 years old to tell Susan about sex, as Susan is not exposed to sexual topics and she has shown no curiosity or interest about sex. Susan is a rare case in American culture, in that she has been largely sheltered from the sexual images and messages in our media, but such cases do exist, and we believe that there is no inherent need to tell a child early on about sex, just for the sake of doing so. Instead, we believe that it is best to wait until the child is developmentally and emotionally ready to learn about sex, unless the child is being exposed to sexual discussions or material in their environment. Unfortunately, most children in America are exposed to sexual material at an early age through TV, as much of the programming contains sexual themes.

We recommend that you answer your child's questions about sex as they come up, and give the amount of information that your child is seeking and is ready to hear. It is important to keep in mind that younger children have shorter attention spans and more limited ability to understand complex concepts. Therefore, it is best to tailor your response based on your child's age and developmental level. For example, if your 5-year-old asks you "Where do babies come from?" you could say, "They come from their mother's body." However, if your 9-year-old child asks the same question, you should explain about sex and pregnancy.

It can be very helpful to use educational books that have been written to teach children about their bodies, puberty, and sex. You can read these books on your own to get ideas about how to present this information to your child, or you can read the book with your child. The key here is to be sure that you talk to your child about sex rather than let them learn about it from others, as the information they get from others may be inaccurate and distorted. Also, research shows that children are less likely to become sexually active at an early age if their parents had already talked with them about sexuality[21].

Here is a list of educational books to help parents talk to their children about sexual issues:

It's Not the Stork!: A Book About Girls, Boys, Babies, Bodies, Families and Friends by Robie Harris (for ages 4 and up)

It's Perfectly Normal: Changing Bodies, Growing up, Sex, and Sexual Health by Robie Harris (for ages 10 and up)

It's So Amazing!: A Book about Eggs, Sperm, Birth, Babies, and Families by Robie Harris (for ages 7 and up)

What's the Big Secret?: Talking about Sex with Girls and Boys by Laurie Krasny Brown and Marc Brown (for ages 4-8)

The "What's Happening to My Body?" Book for Boys: A Growing Up Guide for Parents and Sons by Lynda Madaras and Martin Anderson (for ages 8 to 15)

The "What's Happening to My Body?" Book for Girls: A Growing Up Guide for Parents and Daughters by Lynda Madaras and Marcia Herman-Giddens (for ages 8 to 15)

Is Your Child Ready to Learn About Sex?

Your child may be ready to learn about sex if:

☐ Your child is asking questions about sex
☐ Your child is around other children or older siblings who know about sex
☐ Your child has unrestricted access to TV or the computer, meaning there are no parental controls in place at your child's home or other homes they visit
☐ Your child is displaying sexualized behaviors or making sexual comments
☐ Your child is age 10 or older

Conclusion

It is normal for children to show sexual behaviors, even at a young age. We can think of sexual behaviors as falling along a continuum, from normal to abnormal. In order to evaluate if a child's sexual behaviors are normal, it is important to look at several criteria, as well as the child's age and developmental level. If your child is displaying sexual behaviors that fall out of the normal range, you may want to consider having your child evaluated by a mental health professional who specializes in evaluating sexual behaviors in children. Whether or not your child is showing sexual behaviors, you should be sure to educate your child about genitalia, puberty, and sex.

[1] Reynolds, M.A., Herbenick, D.L., & Bancroft, J. (2003). The Nature of Childhood Sexual Experiences: Two Studies 50 Years Apart, pp. 134-155, in Sexual Development in Childhood, edited by John Bancroft.

[2] Friedrich, W. (1997) Child Sexual Behavior Inventory: Professional Manual, Psychological Assessment Resources.

[3] Volbert, R. (2000). Sexual knowledge of preschool children. *Journal of Psychology and Human Sexuality, 12*(1-2), 5-26.

[4] Friedrich, W. (1997) Child Sexual Behavior Inventory: Professional Manual, Psychological Assessment Resources.

[5] Centers for Disease Control and Prevention (CDC). *1995-2009 Middle School Youth Risk Behavior Survey Data.* Available at http://apps.nccd.cdc.gov/youthonline. Accessed on 4/29/11.

[6] Centers for Disease Control and Prevention (CDC). *1995-2009 Middle School Youth Risk Behavior Survey Data.* Available at http://apps.nccd.cdc.gov/youthonline. Accessed on 4/29/11

[7] Herbenick, D., Reece, M., Schick, V., Sanders, S., Dodge, B., & Fortenberry, D. (2010). Sexual Behavior in the United States: Results from a National Probability Sample of Men and Women Ages 14-94. *Journal of Sexual Medicine, 7* (suppl 5); 255-265.

[8] Fortenberry, JD; Schick, V; Herbenick, D; Sanders, SA; Dodge, B; & Reece, M (2010). Sexual Behaviors and Condom Use at Last Vaginal Intercourse: A National Sample of Adolescents Ages 14 to 17 Years, *Journal of Sexual Medicine, 7*, 305-314.

[9] Herbenick, D., Reece, M., Schick, V., Sanders, S., Dodge, B., & Fortenberry, D. (2010). Sexual Behavior in the United States: Results from a National Probability Sample of Men and Women Ages 14-94. *Journal of Sexual Medicine, 7* (suppl 5); 255-265.

[10] Centers for Disease Control and Prevention (CDC). *1995-2009 Middle School Youth Risk Behavior Survey Data.*

Available at http://apps.nccd.cdc.gov/youthonline.
Accessed on 4/29/11.

[11] Centers for Disease Control and Prevention (CDC). *1995-2009 Middle School Youth Risk Behavior Survey Data.* Available at http://apps.nccd.cdc.gov/youthonline. Accessed on 4/29/11.

[12] National Survey of Sexual Health and Behavior (NSSHB). Findings from the National Survey of Sexual Health and Behavior, Centre for Sexual Health Promotion, Indiana University. *Journal of Sexual Medicine,* Vol. 7, Supplement 5.

[13] Mosher, Chandra & Jones, 2005

[14] Henry Kaiser Family Foundation.(2003). National Survey of Adolescents and Youth Adults: Sexual Health Knowledge, Attitudes and Experiences.

[15] Mosher WD, Chandra A, Jones J. Sexual behavior and selected health measures: Men and women 15–44 years of age, United States, 2002. Advance data from vital and health statistics; no 362. Hyattsville, MD: National Center for Health Statistics. 2005.

[16] Reynolds, M.A., Herbenick, D.L., & Bancroft, J. (2003). The Nature of Childhood Sexual Experiences: Two Studies 50 Years Apart, pp. 134-155, in Sexual Development in Childhood, edited by John Bancroft.

[17] Mosher WD, Chandra A, Jones J. Sexual behavior and selected health measures: Men and women 15–44 years of age, United States, 2002. Advance data from vital and health statistics; no 362. Hyattsville, MD: National Center for Health Statistics. 2005.

[18] Herbenick, D., Reece, M., Schick, V., Sanders, S., Dodge, B., & Fortenberry, D. (2010). Sexual Behavior in the United States: Results from a National Probability Sample of Men and Women Ages 14-94. *Journal of Sexual Medicine,* 7 (suppl 5); 255-265.

[19] Ryan, G. & Blum, J. (1999). Child Sexuality: A Guide for Parents. Kemp Children's Center, Department of Pediatrics, University of Colorado School of Medicine

[20] Gil, E., & Johnson, T. C. (1993). *Sexualized children: Assessment and treatment of sexualized children and children who molest.* Rockville, Maryland: Launch Press.

[21] Bennett, T.F. (2006) *Normal Sexual Development,* in Stewards of Children Facilitator's Manual, Darkness to Light.

Chapter 3: *Effects of Pornography on Children*

Introduction

Rockdale County lies about 15 miles east of Atlanta, and centers on the town of Conyers. The community largely consists of middle class families. One day in the spring of 1996, while the region was preparing to host the upcoming Summer Olympics, a boy went to a community health clinic complaining of various problems. When it was determined that he had the sexually transmitted disease syphilis, he was asked to provide a list of his sexual partners. One of those partners, a young girl, was contacted and asked to provide a list of *her* sexual partners. According to one nurse, it was this girl who provided the "key to our epidemic."

The list of those exposed grew, until it was determined that more than 200 people – most of them teenagers and some as young as 13 – had been exposed. A total of 17 people tested positive for syphilis. Because the victims were so young and came from mostly middle-class homes, the outbreak shocked many. According to a nurse who saw some of the children, "What we were told by a lot of the kids was that there was a lot of sexual activities with multiple partners, a lot of risky sexual activities. These girls were not just having regular intercourse, they were having every kind of possible sexual act that you could do."[1]

The case prompted a documentary by the PBS show *Frontline*, which was called "The Lost Children of Rockdale County." A number of factors that contributed to the case were discovered, in particular that many of the children involved had parents who were mostly uninvolved in their lives and provided little in the way of actual parenting. Another significant factor, however, was pornography. A school guidance counselor recalled hearing stories of "late night sexual games" involving children as young as 12 years old. The counselor remembered one incident in particular that had been related to her, of 10 to 12 kids watching the *Playboy* channel in a girl's bedroom, and playing a game where they had to imitate anything that the adults on screen were doing.[2]

One girl who was interviewed for the documentary talked about participating in a sexual act called a "sandwich," where she performed oral sex on one boy while a second penetrated her vaginally and a third anally.[3] Such an act might seem unthinkable to most adults, but there is one venue where it is practiced with some regularity – pornography. The dynamics between the boys and girls who participated in these activities were fairly well defined. Many of the girls were "passed around" from one boy to another, sometimes having sex with 10 or 20 boys in a night. The boys tended to view the girls with disdain, treating them as disposable objects.[4] This too, is a dynamic commonly found in pornographic movies – the female exists to please the male.

The Rockdale case is a vivid demonstration of the effect that pornography can have on those who view it. There are many people who would think back to their childhood and say that they saw a few *Playboy* magazines or movies and it didn't affect them. Many people would also say that what you watch or view does not affect what you think or do.

To be sure, viewing a particular image or film does not *cause* us to then behave in a similar fashion. There is no question, however, that images can have a powerful *influence* on what we do. In addition, here are some important points to keep in mind:

1) The pornography that children can access today is much more explicit, graphic, and deviant than what we could access when we were children. For example, they can see photos of people performing oral sex on dogs, people being tied up and raped, people cross-dressing, children being molested, and so on.

2) Estimates suggest that up to 90% or more youth between 12 and 18 years old have access to the Internet.[5] Thus, it is much easier for children today to access pornography, and to access it repeatedly, in many different ways. So instead of just stumbling across a *Playboy* magazine left in the woods, today's children can find pornography on cell phones, hand-held videogames, computers, and any other device that can connect to the Internet. *One third* of children ages 11-17 have their own cell phones today; it is projected that *half* will have a cell phone within the next couple of years.[6] Thus, children today are at risk for seeing pornography much more frequently than in the past.

3) There is a fast-growing area of research that shows that exposure to pornography negatively affects both adults and children. We have also found this to be true in our clinical work with children and adults.

How Many Children are Exposed to Pornography?

A number of surveys have been conducted to see how commonplace it is for children to be exposed to pornography. According to a telephone survey[7] of Internet users aged 10 to 17, conducted in 2005:

- 42% of Internet users aged 10 to 17 said they had seen online pornography in a recent 12-month span.
  - Of those users, 66% said the exposure was unwanted.

- Most of the youth who reported unwanted exposure were aged 13 to 17. However, 17% of boys and 16% of girls ages 10 and 11 also had unwanted exposure.

- More than a third of 16 and 17-year-old boys surveyed said they had intentionally visited X-rated sites in the past year. In contrast, only 8% of 16 and 17-year-old girls said they had intentionally visited such sites.

- Overall, 36% of the youth surveyed said they had unwanted exposure to online pornography. This was a 25% increase from a similar survey conducted in 1999 and 2000.

According to an anonymous survey of college students conducted in 2006, 72% of participants had seen online pornography before age 18. More boys reported seeing online pornography before age 18, with 93% of boys and 62% of girls reporting such experience. Most of the exposure began when the youth were ages 14 to 17. Boys were more likely to be exposed to pornography at an earlier age, to see more images, to see more extreme images such as rape and child pornography, and to view pornography more often.

Girls were much more likely to report that they did not intentionally view online pornography. 15% of boys and 8.9% of girls reported having seen sexual pictures of children, demonstrating that exposure to child pornography is more common than most people might think. Overall, these results show just how common it is these days for teens to be exposed to pornography online, including to child pornography. [8]

Most parents realize that their children have seen inappropriate websites. In fact, according to one survey[9], 62% of parents of teens were aware that their children had accessed such websites. And most teens agree that teens do things online that they wouldn't want their parents to know about[10]. Unfortunately, parents cannot assume that their children would tell them if they received a sexual solicitation online, as a study found that almost half of children who received such solicitations did not tell anyone about it[11].

As you can see from these figures, a large percentage of children are exposed to pornography on the Internet. Children may be exposed to pornography accidentally, or they may intentionally seek out pornography. So which children are more at risk?

Which Children are at Highest Risk of Accidentally Seeing Internet Pornography?

Research[12] has found that certain factors made it more likely that a child would accidentally see Internet pornography. Specifically, the children most at risk for accidentally seeing pornography were in their teens, were youth who had reported being harassed or sexually solicited online or interpersonally victimized offline, and youth who scored as having symptoms of depression.

This suggests that as parents, we need to be especially careful in protecting our teens online, as they are at greater risk. This may be because teens are more likely to be rebellious and risk-taking in their behaviors in general, including online. This research also suggests that we as parents need to be especially careful in protecting our children if they have already been harassed online or abused in some way, such as sexually abused. This is not surprising, as there is a lot of research that shows that sexually abused children are at much higher risk than non-abused children of being sexually abused again. The research above also illustrates the need for parents to protect their children who are depressed, and to seek professional help to treat their child's depression.

Children are most likely to be accidentally exposed to pornography in their own home. Specifically, 79% of unwanted youth exposure to pornography occurred in the home[13]. Research also shows that children who use file-sharing programs are at highest risk for accidentally seeing pornography. We have seen many cases where teens used a file-sharing program such as Limewire or Kazaa and they typed in words such as "young," "porn" and "Lolita." For some of these teens, they ended up inadvertently receiving child pornography and were later criminally charged in federal court for possession and/or distribution of child pornography. Children can also accidentally be exposed to pornography through talking online with friends, visiting chat rooms, and playing games on the Internet.

Which Children are More Likely to Seek Out Pornography?

- Boys
  - ➤ In a survey of youth aged 10 to 17, those who sought out pornography, both online and offline, were more likely to be male, with only 5% of seekers being female.[14]
- Teens
  - ➤ 87% of the porn seekers were ages 14 or older[15]
  - ➤ Children under the age of 14 were more likely to report exposure to more traditional types of pornography, such as magazines or movies
- Youth who use file-sharing programs to download images
- Youth who talk online to unknown persons about sex
- Youth who use the Internet at friends' homes

- Youth who have more rule-breaking behaviors in general
  - ➢ Youth who sought out porn were more likely to report delinquent behavior and substance use in the previous year[16]
- Youth who have symptoms of depression and lower levels of emotional bonding with their caregiver or parent. This suggests that you as a parent should be attentive to your child's emotional state, and their emotional connection to you.[17]
- Youth who are high sensation seekers[18]
- Youth who are less satisfied with their lives[19]

All of this suggests that parents need to be most protective of their teenage sons who are depressed, lack a strong emotional attachment to their parents, engage in the high-risk behaviors listed above on the computer, and have behavioral problems. In our clinical practice, we have seen many teens who have developed an addiction to pornography. These teens often have few friends, are emotionally distant from their parents, and have large amounts of unstructured time which they then use to spend hours viewing pornography on the computer. The majority of teens' online use occurs right after school, when working parents are not home.[20] Given this, it may be wise to enroll your teen in an after-school program in order help structure their time with positive, supervised activities.

Is My Child at High Risk for Looking for Porn?

Check if any of the following apply to your child. My child is:

- ☐ Male
- ☐ Age 14 to 17
- ☐ Uses file sharing programs to download images
- ☐ Talks to strangers online about sex
- ☐ Uses the internet at friends' homes
- ☐ Has behavioral problems including delinquent behavior
- ☐ Has used alcohol or drugs within the past year
- ☐ Has symptoms of depression
- ☐ Is not emotionally close to either parent
- ☐ Engages in thrill-seeking behaviors
- ☐ Is dissatisfied with his life

The more items checked, the higher your child's risk for seeking out porn. We recommend trying to address the checked behaviors to reduce your child's risk.

How Does Pornography Affect the Viewer?

Images can have a powerful effect on our perceptions and attitudes. If this weren't the case, the advertising industry would not be spending millions and millions of dollars each year to produce ads designed to get us to buy their products. Film directors such as Alfred Hitchcock took great pride in using images to manipulate audiences and provoke specific feelings. Pornographic images and films are no different, except what is being manipulated there are perceptions and attitudes about sexuality and sexual relationships. Viewing pornography can affect your attitudes about sex, your expectations of others' actions, your perceptions of others' behaviors, and your judgments and behaviors.

For example, if you repeatedly watch pornography that shows rape scenes, you are more likely to view rape as being a normal and acceptable behavior, and are less likely to have empathy for rape victims. This is based on research[21] [22] that shows that men who were briefly exposed to violent pornography were more likely to believe that:

- women are responsible for preventing their own rape
- rapists are normal and should not be severely punished
- women should not resist a rape attack

These men were also:

- less responsive to pain and suffering by rape victims
- more aggressive towards women

Many scenes of rape in pornographic films start out with the woman clearly resisting. As the scene progresses, however, the woman is inevitably overcome with sexual desire and happily participates in the sexual act. Such scenes reinforce the distorted belief that any woman can become a nymphomaniac, provided the male "presses his case" with sufficient force. Needless to say, such attitudes increase the risk of sexual assault, particularly in so-called "date rape" situations where the male insists that the female really "wanted it."

How Does Pornography Affect Children?

Children who view pornography may:

1. Begin displaying sexual behaviors as they try to imitate what they see in the pornography
2. Learn distorted views of sex and relationships
3. Become sexually active at an earlier age

4. Develop deviant sexual interests and sexually aggressive behavior
5. Feel dissatisfied with their own sexual lives
6. Be at higher risk for being sexually abused
7. Be more likely to view pornography and suffer from sexual dysfunctions as an adult
8. Experience negative thoughts and feelings during and after their exposure to the pornography

Let's look at each of these issues in greater depth:

1) **Children who view pornography may begin displaying sexual behaviors as they try to imitate what they see in the pornography.**

One of the ways children learn is by imitating adults. Think of the times when your child has seen you doing something, such as sweeping the floor, and then tried to do the same thing. Children also often imitate what they see on TV – sometimes dangerously, such as trying to fly like their favorite superhero. So it is not surprising then that children would also try to imitate the sexual behaviors they see in pornography. In a study[23] of males and females of junior high school age and above:

- 91% of the males and 82 percent of the females admitted having been exposed to X-rated, hard-core pornography
- Over 66% of the males and 40% of the females reported wanting to try some of the sexual behaviors they had witnessed.
- Among the high schoolers, 31% of the males and 18% of the females admitted actually doing some of the sexual behaviors they had seen in the pornography within a few days after exposure.

In our clinical practice, we have also seen many cases of young children trying to engage in the sexual acts they have seen in pornography. For example, we saw a case of a 10-year-old boy who molested his 3-year-old female cousin after his female neighbor showed him pornographic movies. This boy then licked his cousin's vagina, and he said he did so because he saw it in a movie.

2) **Children who view pornography may learn distorted views of sex and relationships.**

Children learn about relationships by watching others, both in real life and in media. In many cases we have seen, the child's very first exposure to sex and sexual behaviors was not when an adult talked to them about it, or when they received sex education in school, but rather when they first saw pornography. Unfortunately, pornography teaches unhealthy, distorted lessons about people and relationships. It typically depicts people as sex objects, focusing primarily on their breasts and genitals. Or it depicts distorted, unrealistic relationships between people such as a doctor seducing his patient within minutes of meeting her. This teaches children that this is what they should expect in relationships. There are many themes common to pornographic films that children may "learn" are normal behavior, including:

- People are constantly thinking about sex
- It is normal to have sex with strangers
- It is normal to have sex with many different people at once
- Unusual or uncommon sexual practices are actually very common, including anal sex and so-called "double penetration" – where a female has sex with two males and is penetrated vaginally and anally at the same time

- It is commonplace for the girl to resist a sexual advance at first, but inevitably she will come to enjoy and desire it

Research of teens ages 13 to 18[24] showed that the more exposure to online porn, the more likely teens were to have "recreational attitudes" about sex, meaning they view sex as a purely physical function like eating, and feel it isn't necessary to have a relationship with their sexual partner.[25] Boys were much more likely to hold these views than girls, and they tended to hold these attitudes more strongly when they perceived the pornographic material as being a "realistic" depiction of sexual relationships. In addition, boys *and* girls who viewed sexually explicit movies online were more likely to view women as sex objects.[26]

3) **Children who view pornography may become sexually active at an earlier age.**

In a survey of adults, males who had Internet access during the ages of 12 to 17 reported significantly younger ages of first oral sex compared to males without Internet access.[27] In addition, males and females with Internet access, between the ages of 12 and 17, reported younger ages for first sexual intercourse than individuals without Internet access.[28] In our practice, we have seen many children who were exposed to pornography and began having sex at a young age.

4) **Children who view pornography may develop deviant sexual interests and sexually aggressive behavior.**

Children and teens may be particularly affected by pornography, as they are in a developmental stage where their sexual interests are still being formed. Thus, if a child is exposed to pornography showing bondage, a child may develop a sexual interest in bondage. An adult who sees this same pornographic material is less likely to be affected by this, as their sexual interests have likely already been formed years before. However, we have seen cases of adults who developed an interest in child pornography and other deviant pornography after being exposed to it on the Internet. Recent research also suggests that youth who intentionally view violent porn are 6 times more likely to engage in sexually aggressive behavior[29].

In our clinical practice, we have seen many children and teens who have molested younger children after viewing pornography. These children often say that they wanted to try what they had seen in the porn, and they chose a younger child because they thought the younger child would be more likely to go along with it. We have also seen cases where a child developed an interest in a deviant sexual behavior that otherwise they may not have developed. The best example of this is a teenaged girl who viewed images of people molesting animals, and then she molested her own dog. She photographed herself having the dog lick her vagina, and then posted these photos on a bestiality website. Someone from her school found the photos and posted them on a school-related website. The girl was then ostracized and harassed by her peers at school, and her parents became aware of her behavior and withdrew her from school. So, what started out as mere curiosity ended in serious social consequences, not to mention a sexual deviancy problem.

5) **Children who view pornography feel less satisfied with their sex lives.**

In our experience in working with teens who have sexual problems, we have found that the teens' sexual beliefs have been dramatically affected by their exposure to pornography. Research[30] has shown that teens who view Internet pornography more frequently were less satisfied with their sex lives.

It is thought that the teens compared themselves and their sexual experiences to the images in the pornography, and felt inadequate in comparison. Teens with the least sexual experience and fewest sexually experienced peers were most likely to be affected by the exposure to the sexual material. This may be because those teens had less real-life sexual experience to which they could compare what they saw on the Internet. This reminds us of a teenaged boy we saw in therapy who said his first sexual intercourse was very disappointing because it could not live up to the graphic images he had repeatedly seen in pornographic videos online. He said he felt cheated and ended up being angry with the girl for not acting like the girls in the videos.

Feelings of sexual inadequacy can play a role in cases of teens molesting younger children. Teens who view pornography may feel that they cannot hope to match the sexual performance of actors who perform in pornographic films. Males in pornographic films are often depicted as being self-assured, highly confident, and well-endowed. A typical teen viewing such material may end up feeling very inadequate compared to these so-called "role models." This can lead teens to not even attempt to form intimate relationships with peers, and in some cases turn to younger children because they will feel more confident and mature in such a situation.

In our clinical work, we have found that teens who molested young children are often shocked and surprised to learn the average length of a penis. They believed that the penises they saw in pornographic images and films were in fact average and typical. This is understandable, until it is pointed out that one reason the actors in pornography are chosen for those roles is because they tend to be very much above the norm in that department. If we ask these same teens if NBA players are "normal" in terms of height, they are then able to understand the unfair nature of the comparison.

6) **Children who view pornography may be at higher risk for being sexually abused.**

Children who view pornography can become sexualized in their manner, gestures, talk, and behavior. This may inadvertently attract sexual abusers who seek out sexualized children to molest. Offenders are likely to believe (and are often correct) that sexualized children will be easier to manipulate into engaging in sexual behaviors. Offenders who are caught later use this as an excuse, sometimes even accusing the child of being "seductive" and "coming on" to them. Children who view pornography online are at higher risk of being approached by a sexual abuser who is cruising the Internet for victims, such as in chat rooms. See Chapter 5 for more information on how sex offenders manipulate their victims.

7) **Children who view pornography may be at an increased risk of using pornography as an adult and having sexual dysfunctions.**

A recent research study found that early exposure to sexually explicit material is related to later development of sexual dysfunctions as an adult. Thus, children who are exposed to pornography may be more likely to have sexual problems when they grow up.[31] The same study also suggests that children who view pornography are more likely to view pornography as adults. While these researchers have cautioned that their findings are preliminary, their results are consistent with what we have seen in our clinical practice.

We have discussed how children and adolescents can have their sexual attitudes and behaviors shaped by their use of pornography. In some cases, the individual may come to depend upon pornography as their primary sexual outlet, leading them to have sexual problems in any interactions they attempt with actual people. In our clinical practice, we worked with a man who talked about how his pornographic movies became a central focus in his life. He referred to the movies as his "friends," because he could rely on them to make him feel content and happy, if only for a brief period of time. It would be inaccurate to blame this man's sexual offending on his pornography use – there were many factors in his decision to offend – but there is no doubt that his pornography use helped to stunt his sexual development, and thus contributed to his decision to molest a child.

8) **Children who view pornography may experience negative thoughts and feelings during and after their exposure to the pornography.**

Research[32] has shown that teens, particularly female teens, reported having some negative reactions to online pornography. Specifically, 73% of girls reported feeling embarrassed and 51% reported feeling disgusted. Boys, on the other hand, were less likely to report such feelings and were more likely to report feeling sexually excited. However, half of the boys and one third of the girls reported feeling guilt or shame, and about a quarter of the boys and the girls reported having unwanted thoughts about the experience. In our clinical practice, we often hear children and teens talk about having difficulty getting the pornographic images out of their mind, particularly if they viewed such images repeatedly.

What are Parents Doing to Monitor their Children Online?

According to one study[33], most parents try to stay involved in their teenagers' "online lives":

- 65% of parents reported they check the websites their teen visits on a regular basis
- 74% said they can identify whether their teen has created a page on MySpace or Facebook
- 85% of parents reported they have "established rules about the kinds of personal information their child can share with people they talk to on the Internet"
- 68% of parents reported having regulations about which sites their child may visit, and how much time their teen spends online
- 55% of the teens in the study reported that their parents checked to see what websites they had visited.

In a different study[34] of online youth (12–17 years) and parents, the parents of younger teens monitored their children's online behavior more than the parents of older teens. Parents of older teens were less likely to place time limits on their children's Internet use, and were less likely to place monitoring software on the computer. Other research[35] showed that parents believed there were significant online dangers, but they generally did not set limits or monitor their teens' behaviors. The parents also tended to underestimate how much information their teens actually disclosed online. As you might expect, parenting style can have an effect on teens' online behaviors. Research found that teens with authoritative parents engaged in fewer high-risk online behaviors. For example, those teens were less likely to disclose personal information of all kinds online and were less likely to meet online acquaintances in the real world.

An authoritative parenting style refers to parents who are emotionally connected to their children, but who also exercise a lot of control in their children's lives. For more information about the authoritative parenting style versus other parenting styles, see Chapter 8.

We have talked about parental supervision of teens, but what about of young children? One might assume that parents would be especially careful in monitoring their young children's internet access, but research suggests that only 50% of parents watched their Kindergarten and 1st grade students while they interacted with people online.[36] Not surprisingly, 48% of Kindergarten and 1st graders reported viewing online content that made them feel uncomfortable. Many parents seem to think that young children are not capable of finding pornography online or are not likely to run into it, but we have seen many cases of young children accessing porn online, either intentionally or accidentally. All it takes is for an older child or adult to show or tell them about how to type in words into a search engine. It is fairly easy for a 6-year-old to then type in "s-e-x" and access numerous pornographic images.

What Steps Should Parents Take to Prevent Kids' Exposure to Sexual Material?

1) Be aware of the many ways children can gain access to pornography on the Internet, and take steps to make such access more difficult. See Chapter 7 for specific recommendations on how to limit your child's access to pornography on the Internet.

2) Put parental controls on all televisions in the home.

3) Do not put a TV or computer in your child's bedroom so that you can monitor their viewing more easily. There are many TV channels such as the premium movie channels

and even child-oriented channels such as the Cartoon Network that show sexually-themed material at night. For younger children, it may be easiest to control their TV viewing by limiting their viewing to shows on DVD and recorded by TIVO or other digital video recorder that you have already screened for appropriateness.

4) Research TV shows and movies before allowing your child to watch them. For example, you can go to www.commonsensemedia.org or **www.kidsinmind.com** to find out if a certain show contains sexual or violent themes and if it is appropriate for your child's age. While this chapter has focused on pornographic movies and materials, parents should also be mindful of mainstream movies. Many parents would be surprised to discover what certain films actually contain. For example, the DVD packaging for the film "300" would suggest that it is a full-throated action movie. Only in small print on the back does it indicate that the film also contains "some sexuality and nudity." Imagine a mother's shock when she rents "300" for her teenage sons and finds a very graphic scene depicting the protagonist having sex with his wife before he goes off to battle.

5) Make sure that any pornographic materials in your home are in a locked cabinet or safe that your children cannot access.

6) Avoid allowing your child to spend time at other peoples' houses, without your direct supervision, until you have information about whether or not your child might be exposed to pornography in their home. Find out if there are parental controls on the computers and televisions, how any pornographic materials in the home are stored and secured, and what type of adult supervision is provided for the children who visit the home.

7) Work on developing an authoritative parenting style in which you are actively involved in your child's daily life, spend "quality" individual time with your child each day, set limits and establish clear rules about your child's online activity, and monitor your child's online activity. For more information about the authoritative parenting style, see p. 164.

8) Learn more about what your teens are doing on MySpace and other social networking sites. Use these sites yourself so that you are familiar with how they work. Check your child's pages on these sites and review them for appropriateness.

9) Educate your child about the dangers of the Internet, and help them understand that pornography usually does not reflect realistic or healthy sexual relationships.

10) Get your child involved in supervised extracurricular activities and arrange play dates to help them develop face-to-face social relationships as opposed to developing virtual relationships online. Avoid situations where your teenager spends large amounts of unstructured time at home when you are not there, especially if the teen has access to the Internet. One option might be to enroll them in an afterschool program that is well-supervised.

11) Minimize and control your child's time on the Internet, setting a daily limit that you enforce. The American Academy of Pediatrics recommends that children ages 2 and older have no more than one or two hours of screen time in front of a TV or computer per day. You can use various programs to monitor and limit your child's time on the internet, such as programs available at www.kidswatch.com, www.TimesUpKidz.com, www.softwaretime.com.

12) Model appropriate and moderate Internet use for your child in your own use of the Internet, at least in your child's presence.

13) Help your child meet his or her emotional needs through ways other than using the Internet. If your child feels emotionally connected to you and others in his or her life, then your child is less likely to seek an emotional connection with strangers online.

Conclusion

Research and clinical experience have shown that exposure to pornography can have a profound and negative impact on children. Ultimately, it is up to parents to take active steps to protect their children from pornography. Just as parents take steps to not have sex in front of their children, they should make sure their children are not seeing sexual activity through other avenues such as pornography. New technologies make parents' job more difficult as pornography becomes more and more accessible to children, but parents can follow the basic steps above to minimize their children's risk of exposure.

---

[1] *Frontline,* "The Lost Children of Rockdale County," October 19, 1999.
[2] Ibid
[3] Ibid
[4] Ibid
[5] Ybarra, M.L., & Mitchell, K.J., (2005). Exposure to Internet pornography among children and adolescents: A national survey. *Cyberpsychology & Behavior,* 8(5), 473-486.
[6] Barney, S. & Kott, J. (2005). The Porn Standard: Children and Pornography On the Internet. Developed by Third

Way, Washington, DC. Retrieved from
www.thirdway.com.

[7] Wolak, J., Mitchell, K.J., & Finkelhor, D. (2007). Unwanted
and wanted exposure to pornography in a national sample
of youth Internet users. *Pediatrics*, 119(2), 247-257.

[8] Sabina, C; Wolak, J.; Finkelhor, D. *CyberPsychology &
Behavior*, Vol 11(6), Dec 2008, 691-693.

[9] Barney & Kott, 2005

[10] Macgill, A.R. (2007). Parent and teenager Internet use. Pew
Internet & American Life Project,
http://www.pewinternet.org/pdfs

[11] National Center for Missing and Exploited Children

[12] Wolak et al, 2007

[13] Wolak, J., Mitchell, K., & Finkelhor, D. (2006). Online
Victimization of Youth: Five Years Later. National Center
for Missing & Exploited Children.

[14] Ybarra, M.L., & Mitchell, K.J., (2005). Exposure to Internet
pornography among children and adolescents: A national
survey. *Cyberpsychology & Behavior*, 8(5), 473-486.

[15] Ibid

[16] Ibid

[17] Ibid

[18] Peter, J., & Valkenburg, P.M. (2006) Adolescents' exposure
to sexually explicit material on the internet.
Communication Research, 33(2), 178-204.

[19] Ibid

[20] Barney & Kott, 2005

[21] Garcia, L. (1986). Exposure to pornography and attitudes
about women and rape: A correlative study. *Journal of Sex
Research*, 22, 378-385.

[22] Zillman, D. Effects of prolonged consumption of
pornography. In *Pornography: Research Advances and Policy
Considerations*, eds. D. Zillman and J. Bryant (Hillsdale, NJ:
Erlbaum, 1989), 129.

[23] Cline, V. (1990) Pornography's Effects on Adults and Children (New York: Morality in Media), 11.

[24] Peter, J., & Valkenburg, P.M. (2006) Adolescents' exposure to sexually explicit material on the internet. Communication Research, 33(2), 178-204.

[25] Ibid

[26] Peter, J. & Valkenburg, P.M. (2007). Adolescents' exposure to a sexualized media environment and notions of women as sex objects. *Sex Roles*, 56, 381-395.

[27] Kraus, S. & Russell, B.L. (2008). Adolescents' exposure to sexually explicit material and early sexual experiences. *Cyberpsychology & Behavior*, 11(2), 162-168.

[28] Ibid

[29] Ybarra, M., Mitchell, K., Hamburger, M., Diener-West, M., & Leaf, P. (2011). X-rated material and perpetration of sexually aggressive behavior among children and adolescents: Is there a link? *Aggressive Behavior*, 37 (1), 1-18.

[30] Peter, J., & Valkenburg, P.M. (2006) Adolescents' exposure to sexually explicit internet material and sexual satisfaction: A longitudinal study. *Human Communication Research*. 33 (2). 178-204.

[31] Hunt, S. & Kraus, W. (2009). *Sexual Addiction and Compulsivity*,16 (1), 79-100.

[32] Sabina, C; Wolak, J.; Finkelhor, D. (2008). *CyberPsychology & Behavior*, 11(6), 691-693.

[33] Macgill, A.R. (2007). Parent and teenager Internet use. Pew Internet & American Life Project, http://www.pewinternet.org/pdfs

[34] Wang, R., Bianci, S., & Raley, S. (2005). Teenagers' Internet use and family rules: A research note. *Journal of Marriage and Family*, 67, 1249-1258.

[35] Rosen, L., Cheever, N., & Carrier, L.M. (2008). The association of parenting style and child age with parental limit setting and adolescent MySpace behavior. *Journal of Applied Developmental Psychology*, 29(6), 459-471.

[36] McQuade, S. & Sampat, N. (2008). Survey of internet and at-risk behaviors. Rochester Institute of Technology.

Chapter 4: *Sexual Abuse and Its Effect on Children*

What is Sexual Abuse?

While most of us have a general idea of what sexual abuse involves, it is helpful to define the parameters of sexual abuse, as it can include a wide range of behaviors. In a nutshell, sexual abuse includes involving a child in sexual practices that:

- violate laws or social taboos

- the child does not fully understand, and

- the child is unable to consent to

There are different types of sexual abuse such as sexual contact between an adult and child under age 16, underage prostitutes, children involved in pornography, exposing children to pornography, and exposing children to nudity or sexual activity for an adult's sexual gratification. Physical discipline that involves nudity, such as making a child strip naked and then whipping the child, may also constitute sexual abuse. It can also result in the child associating nudity and/or sexual arousal with pain. Such associations can later result in the child developing an interest in sexual sadism (being sexually aroused by causing others pain) or sexual masochism (being sexually aroused by oneself being in pain or being made to suffer). In our practice, we have worked with many individuals who were whipped while nude and later developed these deviant sexual interests.

All of these forms of sexual abuse have one thing in common – they involve a violation of the child's boundaries for someone else's sexual gratification. Sexual abusers often begin the abuse by slowly violating the child's boundaries. For example, the abuser may walk around nude in front of the child, shower with the child, sleep in bed with the child, or kiss the child on the lips. The abuser slowly gets the child used to small boundary violations so the child is less likely to react negatively or to question the later, larger violations of boundaries. For example, the abuser might initially cuddle in bed with the child while both of them are fully clothed, but later progress to cuddling in bed with the child while they are both nude.

With young children, it can sometimes be difficult to determine when an adult's behavior is just part of normal caretaking or when it is a possible sign of sexual abuse. The key is to determine if the adult's behavior is motivated by sexual reasons or not. Adult nudity in and of itself is not likely to be damaging to a young child, if the nudity occurs in the process of changing clothes, bathing, showering, or other natural behaviors where there is no sexual motivation. However, poor boundaries in the home may contribute to the child displaying sexualized behaviors, showing poor boundaries with others, and experiencing anxiety.

When is Adult Nudity and Showering with Children Inappropriate?

Many of us would agree that it is normal and acceptable for young children to sometimes see their parents' nudity. Many of us would also agree that parents need to help their young children with washing their children's bodies, wiping them after they use the toilet, and applying medicine to their genitals. However, part of a child's healthy development involves learning appropriate boundaries and a sense of privacy. The question then becomes when should parents change their caretaking practices?

Based on a survey[1] of American mental health and child welfare professionals, we recommend that parents consider stopping certain practices when their child reaches a particular age. These ages differ depending on whether the parent is a mother or father, and whether the child is a son or daughter. Generally speaking, it is recommended that parents stop these practices at earlier ages when their child is of the opposite sex. For example, we recommend that fathers stop taking baths with their daughters when their daughters are 2 years old as opposed to stopping this behavior with their sons when their sons are 3 years old.

The following tables list the recommended ages for when parents should consider stopping certain practices. These ages are based on the median ages from the survey of mental health and child welfare professionals noted above. There was a wide range of opinion among the professionals so we chose to list the median age, which is the middle of the ages reported by the professionals. This means that about half of the professionals thought the practice should stop at a younger age while the other half thought the practice should stop at an older age. However, most of the professionals agreed that the practice should stop within 2 to 3 years of the ages listed in the tables, depending on the specific practice.

If a parent continues these practices beyond the recommended ages listed below, this does not necessarily mean the parent is being inappropriate with the child. The main criterion in determining if the behavior is inappropriate is whether or not the adult is engaging in the behavior for sexual purposes. However, the following recommended ages do provide a general guideline for setting healthy boundaries with children.

Recommended Ages for Fathers to Stop Certain Parenting Practices:

	With Sons	With Daughters
Hygiene Behaviors		
Taking baths together	Age 3	Age 2
Taking showers together	Age 3	Age 3
Wiping child after using toilet	Age 4	Age 4
Washing child's body	Age 5	Age 4
Applying medicine to child's private parts	Age 5	Age 5
Affection Behaviors		
Kissing child on the mouth	Age 5	Age 5
Giving child back & neck rubs	Age 8	Age 8
Privacy Behaviors		
Adult being naked around child	Age 4	Age 4
Child seeing parent use toilet	Age 4	Age 3
Child sleeping with single parent	Age 5	Age 5
Parent & child changing together (including underwear)	Age 5	Age 4

Parents may need to continue some of these practices if their child still needs help in certain areas, such as with thoroughly wiping themselves after using the toilet or washing themselves in the shower. For example, children with intellectual limitations or delayed development often need their parents' help with hygiene behaviors well past the age that other children need such help. When trying to decide if you should stop a certain practice, ask yourself, "can my child do this on his own?" and "how can I help my child progress toward being able to do this on his own?" The goal, of course, is to help your child be able to take care of their own hygiene as soon as the child is able to do so.

Recommended Ages for Mothers to Stop Certain Parenting Practices:

	With Sons	With Daughters
Hygiene Behaviors		
Taking baths together	Age 3	Age 3
Taking showers together	Age 3	Age 4
Wiping child after using toilet	Age 4	Age 4
Washing child's body	Age 5	Age 5
Applying medicine to child's private parts	Age 5	Age 6
Affection Behaviors		
Kissing child on the mouth	Age 5	Age 5
Giving child back & neck rubs	Age 8	Age 8
Privacy Behaviors		
Adult being naked around child	Age 4	Age 1
Child seeing parent use toilet	Age 3	Age 4
Child sleeping with single parent	Age 5	Age 5
Parent & child changing together (including underwear)	Age 5	Age 5

This survey also asked mental health and child welfare professionals if it is acceptable for children to be in the same room when parents are engaging in sexual relations. As you might expect, about 80% of the respondents indicated this practice this was never acceptable. And among those who thought it was acceptable, it was recommended the practice stop when the child is young, at around 2 to 2 ½ years old.

Should parents lock their bedroom door when having sex? Yes. 72% of the professionals surveyed indicated that parents *should* lock their bedroom doors[2]. So, the message here is that it is generally not acceptable to have sex in front of your child or with your bedroom door unlocked, as your child could walk in. Parents often assume that they do not need to lock their door if their child is asleep. However, we have seen many cases where children woke up at night, walked into their parents' room, and saw the parents' sexual activity, oftentimes without the parents even knowing. Given this risk, we recommend that you routinely lock your bedroom door when having sex, regardless of the time of day.

How Common is Sexual Abuse?

Sexual abuse is much more common than most people realize. Studies show that 1 in 4 girls[3] and 1 in 6 boys are sexually abused before the age of 18. And, more than 20% of children are sexually abused before the age of 8.[4] Sadly, children are the main targets of sexual abusers. Nearly 70% of all sexual assaults, including assaults on adults, occur to children ages 17 and under. In addition, children under age 12 make up nearly half of all victims of forcible sodomy, sexual assault with an object, and forcible fondling.[5] [6]

Who is at Highest Risk for Being Sexually Abused?

Girls are at about 2 ½ to 3 times higher risk than boys

for being sexually abused. However, approximately 22% to 29% of all child sexual abuse victims are male.[7] A child's risk for being sexually abused generally rises as he or she gets older:

- about 10% of sexual abuse victims are age 3 and under
- 28.4% are ages 4 to 7
- 25.5% are ages 8 to 11
- 35.9% are ages 12 and older[8]

Children who have one or more parent absent from their lives are at higher risk of being sexually abused.[9] Girls who have a stepfather in their home are at double the risk of being sexually abused. This includes risk of abuse by the stepfather, as well as risk of abuse by other men before the arrival of the stepfather in the home.[10] Studies have also found that parental problems, especially maternal illness or alcoholism, extended maternal absences, serious marital conflicts, parental substance abuse, social isolation, and punitive parenting have been associated with increased risk of sexual abuse.[11] We have found this to be true in our own clinical experience. For example, we have seen many cases of girls being sexually abused by their mother's boyfriends or new husbands. Concerned parents can reduce this risk by being careful about who they allow to be alone with their child, even if it is a seemingly trustworthy boyfriend.

Who Are the Abusers?

People often assume that child molesters are strangers who abduct and molest children. However, only 10% of sexual abuse victims are abused by strangers. In fact, 30-40% of sexual abuse victims are abused by a family member[12,13,14] and 50% of are abused by someone outside of the family whom they know and trust. When convicted child molesters were surveyed, 91.8% of them reported that they molested children they know. Only 8.2% of child molesters targeted strangers.[15]

People also often assume that child molesters are adults. However, approximately 40% of sexual abuse victims were abused by older or larger children whom they knew.[16] Thus, parents need to be careful not only about adults, but also about other children that their children are exposed to.

> *Sexual abuse is usually committed by someone the child knows well.*

How Will I Know if My Child Has Been Sexually Abused?

The best approach is to ask your child directly if someone has touched him or her on the private parts. However, children often do not tell when they have been sexually abused. Therefore, it is important to pay attention to any changes in your child's behavior, as such changes could reflect abuse. Keep in mind, though, that changes in your child could be related to other stressors such as a recent move, divorce, or social rejection by peers. Therefore, it is important to consider all of the potential stressors that could be affecting your child.

> *Many sexually abused children were molested by older or larger children rather than by adults*

Does My Child Show Signs of Sexual Abuse?

Look for recent changes in your child that do not seem related to any recent stressors such as:

Changes in Behavior:

☐ Wetting or soiling oneself
☐ Having sleep problems or nightmares
☐ Withdrawing from others
☐ Having difficulty concentrating
☐ Showing a drop in grades
☐ Having angry outbursts
☐ Engaging in self-harming behaviors such as cutting
☐ Talking about sexual things
☐ Drawing pictures with sexual themes
☐ Showing unusual or excessive sexual behaviors

Changes in Emotions:

☐ Having mood swings   ☐ Being anxious or fearful
☐ Being depressed   ☐ Being afraid of the dark

Physical Changes:

☐ Repeated vaginal or urinary infections
☐ Redness, irritation or injury to the child's genitals
☐ Frequent, unexplained constipation
☐ Changes in appetite or significant weight loss or weight gain
☐ Physical symptoms such as stomachaches or headaches that have no medical basis

Do Abused Children Usually Disclose the Abuse?

No. In fact, most abuse goes unreported. Estimates suggest that only 3% of all cases of child sexual abuse[17] and only 12% of rapes involving children are ever reported to police[18]. And only 2 to 8% of incest victims reported their sexual victimization[19]. A national survey of over 3,000 women found that of those raped during childhood, 47% did not disclose to anyone for over 5 years after the rape. In fact, 28% of the women reported that they had *never* told anyone about their childhood rape prior to the research study. Furthermore, the women who never told often suffered the most serious abuse. For instance, they were often younger age at the time of the rape, had a familial relationship with the perpetrator, or had experienced a series of rapes[20].

Why Do Some Children Not Tell?

Many children do not tell about being sexually abused because they assume that they will get in trouble for the abuse. The children believe this because abusers often tell them that there will be negative consequences if they tell. For example, the abuser may tell the child that her family will be ripped apart or that she will be sent to foster care if she tells. The abuser may also threaten to harm the child or her family if the child tells. However, many abusers are able to manipulate the child into silence without using overt threats. Abusers often slowly manipulate the child into sexual contact over time, so the child does not initially realize what is happening. Over time, the abuser begins to violate more and more boundaries, and the child eventually realizes that something is wrong. However, by the time the child realizes this, she often feels like it is too late to tell, and that people won't understand why she didn't tell sooner. The child may also believe that others will blame her, saying she went along with the abuse. The child herself may feel guilty and believe that she is somehow responsible for the abuse. Some abusers induce this guilt by telling the child things such as "you know you wanted it" and "you were asking for it." However, many sexually abused children feel guilty and responsible for the abuse, even if their abuser did not make such statements. Children are generally taught to respect adults and their decisions, so if an adult abuses a child, the child may assume she must have done something to deserve such treatment. The child may then believe that she is bad, resulting in shame and low self-esteem. Many sexually abused children do not disclose their abuse because they are ashamed about the abuse and are worried what others will think of them.

Boys seem to have a particularly difficult time dealing with sexual abuse and are less likely to report it than girls. Studies show that 42% to 85% of sexually abused men did not tell anyone about their history of sexual abuse[21]. Also, studies show that the more severe the abuse, the more likely the boy is to blame himself and the less likely he will disclose the abuse[22]. Boys may also be reluctant to tell about any sexual abuse for fear that others will accuse them of lying about the allegations, reject them, tease them, or accuse them of being gay.

How Does Sexual Abuse Affect the Child?

There is no simple to answer to this question, as sexual abuse can affect children in many different ways. Some children may show no problems as a result of the abuse while others may show severe problems. Children may also show no symptoms at first, but may develop problems over time. In fact, as many as one fourth of sexually abused children may report or show no problems within 2 years of the abuse. However, research shows that those children who initially had no symptoms had more problems 18 months later[23]. Thus, we cannot assume that a child has not been negatively affected by abuse just because the child does not show immediate symptoms. In fact, we have seen many cases where sexually abused children seemed fine after the abuse, but later developed major problems, especially when going through puberty. Since puberty involves the child maturing physically and experiencing sexual feelings, it can trigger memories of past sexual abuse that have lay dormant for years. This can then result in anxiety, confusion, shame, and other negative feelings coming to the surface.

What Determines How a Child Will React?

How a child reacts to sexual abuse depends on many factors such as 1) the frequency and severity of the abuse, 2) the nature of the child's relationship with the abuser, 3) the child's perception of the abuse, and 4) how others respond to the discovery of the abuse.

Child's relationship to abuser:

Children who are molested by parents, loved ones, or trusted caretakers may be especially confused by the abuse. The child may have difficulty understanding how someone who supposedly loves him is then doing things that make him uncomfortable. The child, especially a young child, may assume that the sexual activity is a normal part of a child's relationship with an adult, especially if the child has never been educated about appropriate versus inappropriate touching. The abuser may tell the child things to reinforce this belief such as, "this is how I show you love" and "all daddies do this with their daughters." The child may then try to engage in similar sexual behaviors with other adults,

assuming that this is what is expected. The child may feel
confused and ashamed when an adult reacts in horror to their
sexualized behavior. In fact, sexual abuse of young children is
often discovered when the child acts out sexually without
realizing that her behavior is inappropriate. For example:

> 4-year-old Ashley's daddy coaxed her into sucking his penis,
> so she believes that this is what daughters do with their daddies.
> Ashley later asks her uncle if she can suck his "wee wee." When
> asked where she learned this, Ashley reveals that daddy taught her
> this. Ashley has learned that this is what you do to show love, and
> this distorted belief can affect her for the rest of her life. She may feel
> that she needs to engage in sexual activity with others to show that
> she loves them, or for them to love her. She may also learn that
> people close to you can trick you, and are not to be trusted, as her
> daddy tricked her.

Thus, sexual abuse can affect the child's view of
relationships and can undermine her trust in others. Ashley
could also react to the abuse by developing arousal to a power
dynamic in sexual relationships. In other words, she may
later repeat the power dynamic that she experienced with her
father, in her fantasies or relationships with others. For
example, she may try to trick other children into sexual
contact with her and may be aroused by manipulating others
into sexual activity. Older children, who know intellectually
that sexual abuse is not normal, may assume that there must
be something wrong with them for their caretaker to be doing
such things to them. This can result in the child feeling like
they are bad or somehow deserving of the abuse. The child
may also feel like they are "damaged goods" as a result of the
abuse, and may assume that no one will want them because of
the abuse they have experienced.

Other children may respond to the abuse by internalizing the messages from their perpetrator, whatever those messages are. For example, if the perpetrator repeatedly tells the child, "you know you're sexy, you want it, you little slut," the child may come to view herself as a sex object, and she may grow up to be promiscuous. When the abuser is a loved one or parent, it is often more difficult for the child to hate the abuser or to dismiss what the abuser tells them. This can be because the child loves the abuser and/or because the abuser has greater access to the child and repeats the negative messages over and over. It may also be easier for a child to overcome abuse by a stranger or non-relative, as that abuse generally does not involve the same level of emotional betrayal by a loved one. It can be very difficult for a child to understand how their father or loved one could molest them and betray their trust. This can result in the child feeling like he can never trust anyone, especially those who are close to him.

Child's perception of the abuse:

In our years of working with abused children, we have been struck by how differently children can perceive sexual abuse. We have learned to never make assumptions about how a child feels about his or her history of sexual abuse. Some children may view the abuse as frightening and painful, while others may not even realize that they are being abused. The child's perception depends, at least in part, on how the abuser treats the child before, during and after the abuse. If the abuser uses force and threats, the child can typically identify that the abuse is wrong and that this person is not to be trusted. This is very different from an abuser who is nice to the child and slowly manipulates the child into the abuse by offering extra attention, treats and privileges. The child who is physically forced into the abuse is more likely to dislike their perpetrator and to recognize that they were victimized. In contrast, the child who is manipulated into the abuse may not view the abuse as clearly wrong, and may actually identify with the abuser and try to protect him from getting in trouble. There is also research that suggests that a male victim who idolizes his perpetrator is at greater risk for becoming a perpetrator himself. For example, if Joey was molested by his favorite uncle, who he looks up to, then Joey is at higher risk for becoming a perpetrator. Of course there are other important factors that affect whether or not a victim becomes a perpetrator. This will be discussed later in this chapter.

How others respond to the discovery of the abuse:

Sexually abused children are typically greatly affected by how those around them respond when the abuse is discovered. This is not surprising, given that children's view of the world is generally shaped by what they learn from others in their immediate environment. For example, if a child is raised in a sexist and racist home, the child is likely to develop sexist and racist views. The same is true regarding views of sexual abuse. For example, we have seen many cases where there has been incest in multiple generations of a family, and the family believes that incest is acceptable and to be expected. In cases like this, we often see sexually abused children who are resigned to being abused, and they view the abuse as part of life. That is not to say that these children are not affected by the abuse. Instead, they are less likely to have insight into how the abuse has affected them, which can make it more difficult for them to heal from the abuse. We believe that this also places them at higher risk for unwittingly marrying perpetrators in the future, and possibly for becoming perpetrators themselves.

It appears to be extremely important how the child's mother responds when sexual abuse is discovered. Research shows that if the child's mother does not believe the child's allegations, the child is more likely to have emotional and behavioral problems[24][25]. This makes sense, as the child realizes that he or she cannot count on their mother to believe them and protect them. This is understandably very upsetting to a child. Sadly, we have seen many cases where the mother chooses to believe her husband or boyfriend over her child, and chooses to stay with the abuser. The child often either continues to be abused, or if the authorities are notified, the child is taken into foster care. When the latter happens, the child often becomes depressed and/or angry. In contrast, children whose mothers were supportive and believed their disclosures, tend to show fewer emotional and behavioral problems, and are often able to heal more quickly from the abuse.

How Do Children Usually Cope with Sexual Abuse?

Different children cope with sexual abuse in different ways. Some children may deny that the abuse is happening, acting as if nothing is wrong. They may think that if they pretend that everything is fine, then everything will be fine. These children try to block out the painful reality by daydreaming or repressing the memories. It can be difficult to tell if this child is being abused, as the child spends a lot of mental energy trying to present as if everything is fine. However, this type of child may have attention problems in school and present as being "spacey."

Some sexually abused children may withdraw from others and their environment. These children may appear depressed and quiet. Other children may respond to sexual abuse by acting out in anger. These children may show behavioral problems at home and school. Still other children may respond to abuse by trying to be perfect and seeking approval from others. These children may be successful in school and other areas of their lives, thereby masking their underlying pain.

Which Sexually Abused Children Experience the Most Problems?

The sexually abused children who experience the most problems are those who:

- were molested at a very young age
- experienced extended and frequent abuse
- were molested by a biological parent
- were molested in a forceful manner
- were molested by multiple perpetrators
- had a caretaker who denied that the abuse occurred[26]

Thus, we would expect a child who was forcibly sexually abused at a young age, by relatives and more than one perpetrator, to be experiencing significant emotional and/or behavioral problems, particularly if her mother did not believe the abuse occurred. However, it is important to keep in mind that not all children have the same reaction to abuse. The child's reaction appears to be somewhat related to the child's personality and genetics. For example, a child who is already somewhat anxious and has a family history of anxiety disorders may be more prone to develop Posttraumatic Stress Disorder (a type of anxiety disorder in response to trauma) than a child who does not have such a history of anxiety[27].

What Types of Problems Can Sexually Abused Children Develop?

Emotional Problems:

Research shows that sexually abused children have higher rates of depression and anxiety. They also have lower self-esteem and symptoms of Post-traumatic Stress Disorder[28]. PTSD is a disorder that a person can develop in response to a major trauma. Many people have heard of PTSD in relation to war veterans who were traumatized by their combat experience and later experience flashbacks. However, people can develop PTSD in response to any trauma, not just war. PTSD involves the individual:

1) re-experiencing the trauma through flashbacks, nightmares, intrusive thoughts or memories

2) avoiding things associated with the trauma

3) having persistent symptoms of increased arousal such as:

- difficulty sleeping
- irritability
- difficulty concentrating
- exaggerated startle response
- hypervigilance (being overly alert to their environment as they search for signs of danger)

Children with PTSD may be nervous, jumpy, appear "spacey," have difficulty sleeping, show unusual fears, and be afraid of separating from their caregiver.

Behavioral Problems:

Many sexual abuse victims have unresolved anger. As

a result, they may have problems with chronic irritability and uncontrollable feelings of anger. They may internalize the anger as self-hatred and depression, or externalize and act out against others. Sexually abused children often display behavioral problems such as fighting, bullying, and attacking other children. Compared to non-abused girls, sexually abused adolescent girls are more likely to run away from home, develop substance abuse problems, be bulimic, and have problems with their teachers[29]. Sexually abused girls also have lower self-esteem, more internalized aggression, and poorer relationships with their mothers.

Sexual Problems:

As discussed previously, sexually abused children show more sexualized behaviors than other children and other types of abused children. For example, 4-year-old boys who have been sexually abused are much more likely to fondle another child's genitals, than are 4-year-old boys who have not been sexually abused. In fact, fondling is 6.2 times more common among the preschool age boys who have been sexually abused. Sexually abused children also tend to engage in sexual behaviors associated with genital sexual activity such as mimicking intercourse and inserting objects into their anus or vagina. For example, attempted intercourse is 40 times more common among sexually abused preschool age boys than among their non-abused counterparts, and 9 times more common among the sexually abused girls.

Sexually abused children who have suffered severe abuse are more likely to show sexual behaviors, as are those children who were molested by more than one perpetrator. Also, children who experienced sexual abuse involving threats or force are more likely to show sexual behaviors.

Although sexually abused children are more likely to show sexual behaviors than non-abused children, not all sexually abused children display sexualized behaviors. In fact, only one third of sexually abused children display sexualized behaviors and less than 1% of sexually abused children go on to molest other children. Here is an example of a child who did go on to molest others:

> *Joe is a 7-year-old boy who was physically and sexually abused by his mother's boyfriend. Joe was placed in foster care and he then molested his 4-year-old brother by fondling his brother's penis and performing oral sex on him. Joe also masturbated compulsively, sometimes in front of others. Joe was so compulsive in his sexual acting out that he would molest his younger brother during the short time that his foster mother would leave to use the bathroom. Joe also found ways to get around the alarm on his bedroom door so he could molest his brother at night. In addition to sexual acting out, Joe was depressed and physically aggressive toward others. He had to be moved to a different home because he kept molesting his younger brother despite counseling and despite a safety plan. He then sexually propositioned two teenage girls in his next placement. He was finally stabilized once he was placed in home with no other children.*

In addition to showing sexual behaviors, sexually abused children are at higher risk for becoming pregnant. Research shows that sexually abused children and adolescents have significantly higher rates of pregnancy than their non-abused peers.[30] Sexually abused children are also at higher risk for becoming a prostitute later in life. Research shows that 66% of all prostitutes were sexually abused as children.[31]

Interpersonal Problems:

Sexually abused children often have problems in their

relationships with others. Research shows that sexually abused children tend to be more aggressive and more socially withdrawn, with poorer social skills than their peers. They also tend to feel different from other people and tend to be less trusting of others. This is not surprising, given that their abuser may have socially isolated them from their others, they have experienced a trauma that many others have not experienced, and their abuse has taught them that others cannot be trusted.

Lack of Healthy Coping:

Sexually abused children may have difficulty coping with negative feelings and they may use unhealthy coping strategies. For example, they abuse drugs or alcohol in an attempt to "numb" themselves when they are having negative feelings. They may also cut their arms, wrists or legs when they feel overwhelmed or depressed.

Cognitive Problems:

Research shows that sexually abused children tend to have academic difficulties in school. They also often have distorted beliefs. For example, they often view themselves as being helpless and blame themselves for bad things that happen.

Re-victimization:

Sadly, sexually abused children are at higher risk for being victimized again. In fact, sexually abused children are more likely to be the victims of rape or to be involved in physically abusive relationships as adults. Specifically, individuals who were sexually abused as children are almost 2 ½ to 3 times more likely than non-abused individuals to be sexually assaulted as adults[32]. In addition, those individuals with more severe childhood abuse were more likely to be abused again as adults and were more likely to have more severe sexual assault experiences in adulthood. Also, victims with more symptoms of posttraumatic stress are at higher risk for being sexually assaulted again.[33]

There are many theories that attempt to explain why sexual abuse victims are at higher risk for being sexually assaulted again. These theories suggest that victims develop dysfunctional ways to regulate their emotions such as dissociation, substance abuse, numbing, and compulsive sexual behavior. Perpetrators may pick up on these symptoms or behaviors and may then target these individuals. These symptoms and behaviors may also impair the victim's ability to sense danger and to protect themselves.

What Are the Long-Term Effects of Sexual Abuse?

Research over the past 30 years indicates that sexually abused individuals are more likely to have psychological and interpersonal problems as adults than those who were not sexually abused. These problems include clinical depression, Borderline Personality Disorder, substance abuse, Post-traumatic Stress Disorder, and Bulimia[34]. Some of the long-term problems may actually be related to changes in the person's brain as a result of the abuse. Research suggests that child abuse and neglect can lead to abnormalities in the brain that affect mood and the ability to regulate mood, fear, and anxiety. Thus, trauma can impair someone's ability to maintain emotional balance. Patients with a history of childhood abuse were twice as likely to have an abnormal EEG. These abnormalities were associated with increased aggression and self-destructive behavior. Research also suggests that abused patients have deficient development of the left hemisphere. These deficits may contribute to the development of depression.

Abuse victims often repeat the cycle of abuse with their own children. For example, research shows that teenage mothers who were sexually abused are more likely to abuse their children or have them taken by Child Protective Services due to some type of abuse or neglect. Sexual abuse victims are also more likely to unwittingly marry perpetrators who then molest their children. If the mother was not believed when she disclosed her own history of childhood sexual abuse, then she is likely to respond similarly, in disbelief, when her own child discloses sexual abuse. Thus, the cycle of abuse often continues from generation to generation. Consider the case of Brittany:

Brittany was sexually abused as a young child by her biological father, and her mother did not believe Brittany when she disclosed the abuse. Brittany went on to molest several young children. After her own sexual offending was discovered, Brittany was taken into foster care and placed in a psychiatric hospital for sexually aggressive girls. While in the hospital, she molested a younger girl who was on her unit. Brittany was charged with Sexual Battery and sent to juvenile detention for a year. After serving her time, she returned to residential treatment for 3 years. Despite years of treatment, she denied having a sexual problem, often threatened to run away, and solicited adult male strangers for sex. She had severe psychological problems including mood swings, impulsive behavior, and trying to kill herself. At age 18, she became pregnant by a much older man who later molested their child. Brittany did not believe the abuse occurred and so her child ended up in foster care just as Brittany had.

How Can Children Heal From Sexual Abuse?

It appears that sexually abused children do best when they disclose their abuse and their caretakers believe their allegations and provide emotional support. Ideally, the caretaker should allow the child to openly talk about the abuse and their feelings, without pressuring the child to talk.

However, this can be difficult for both the child and caretaker, particularly if the abuse occurred in the family. For example, the child may feel ashamed to talk about the abuse and the caretaker may not want to hear the details, as it may be too upsetting. It may also bring back negative memories for the caretaker if he or she was molested as a child. For these and many other reasons, it is recommended that sexually abused children receive counseling to help process their thoughts and feelings about the abuse. It is best to choose a counselor who has specific training in treating sexually abused children. Such a counselor should be trained in therapy techniques that have been shown to be effective in treating sexual abuse. For example, Trauma Focused Cognitive Behavioral Therapy is a specific treatment model designed to treat trauma. For more information about this model, go to http://www.modelprograms.samhsa.gov/pdfs/model/TFCBT.pdf

Many parents hope that their children will "forget" about the abuse and they worry that talking about the abuse in therapy will keep reminding the child of the abuse. It is true that the child will probably be asked to talk about the abuse in therapy. However, talking about the abuse should help your child work through their feelings about the abuse so the child can heal from the abuse. Talking about the abuse is likely to be uncomfortable for the child and caretaker, but this is an important part of the healing process. Here is an analogy that we often use with our clients to help them understand the process of counseling. Imagine that you get a splinter in your foot. If you never remove the splinter, it will remain under the skin. It can get infected and cause even more pain. Or, you may forget about the splinter and it may even stop hurting, but it is still there. Healing from abuse is like removing a splinter from your foot. It hurts to stick a needle

in your foot and remove the splinter, but this is a necessary
step in the healing process.

Therapy for sexual abuse typically involves first
learning skills for managing stress and anxiety, and then
gradually talking about the abuse, at a pace that is
comfortable for the client. Therapy may involve different
ways of helping the client express his or her feelings about the
abuse such as through art or journaling. Clients may also be
asked to write a letter to their abuser expressing their feelings,
although the letter is often not mailed. Instead, it is a
therapeutic exercise to help the client express their feelings.

Can the Family Be Reunified After Incest?

When sexual abuse is discovered in the home, the
abuser is often required by Child Protective Services or law
enforcement to leave the home. This is generally
recommended, particularly for abusers who are teens or
adults. Families can be reunified after sexual abuse has
occurred in the family, assuming that the sexual abuse is
adequately addressed in counseling and assuming that
reunification is in the abused child's emotional best interest.
Reunification is not recommended in cases where the abuser,
abused child, and/or the family:

- deny the abuse occurred
- refuse to address the sexual abuse in treatment
- are unwilling to follow a safety plan to ensure the
  abused child is never left alone with the abuser

Reunification is also not recommended if the abuser's
risk for reoffending is too high for him or her to live in the
same home with the child he abused, or if the abused child
feels unsafe living with the abuser. Ideally, before
reunification is considered, the following should occur:

1) the abused child should receive individual counseling to help her process her thoughts and feelings about the sexual abuse
2) the abuser should attend and complete a sex offender treatment program
3) the family should receive family therapy to address the sexual abuse and the family dynamics that may have contributed to the abuse
4) the abused child and abuser have a "clarification" therapy session together in which the abuser apologizes to the child, takes full responsibility for his behavior, and the child has the chance to ask the abuser questions.

Assuming all of these steps go well, the abused child then typically begins having short supervised visits with the abuser. Assuming these visits go well, the visits become more frequent and longer, progressing to overnight visits. It is very important that the family follow a safety plan to ensure that the abused child is supervised at all times around the abuser, to decrease the risk of the abuse occurring again. Assuming the overnight visits go well, the visits may expand to weekend visits and eventually result in the abuser moving back into the home with the child. However, it is recommended that both the child and abuser continue to attend counseling for at least several months after the reunification, to ensure that the reunification process is going smoothly. Specifically, ongoing counseling can assess if the child feels safe, the safety plan is being followed, and the abuser is able to manage his high-risk thoughts and feelings that could lead to reoffense.

There is no set timeline for the reunification process, as it depends on how the victim, abuser, and family respond to treatment. However, sex offender treatment of teens or adults typically takes a year or more. Thus, reunification is typically not recommended for at least a year in those cases. Families often want to rush the reunification process, as they are eager for their families to reunite. However, rushing the process is not recommended, especially since it places pressure on the victim and can result in premature reunification and the abuser reoffending.

Conclusion

Sexual abuse can affect children in many different ways, such that not all children are affected the same way. How a child is affected by abuse depends on the many factors such as the frequency and severity of the abuse, the nature of the child's relationship with the abuser, the child's perception of the abuse, and how others respond to the discovery of the abuse. The good news is that counseling and emotional support following the abuse can greatly help the child cope with the sexual abuse in a healthy manner, and can decrease the child's distress.

---

[1] Johnson, T.C.; Hooper, R. (2003). Boundary and Family Practices: Implications for Assessing Child Abuse. *Journal of Child Sexual Abuse.* Vol 12 (3/4) 103-126.

[2] Johnson, T.C. Family Practices Questionnaire II data, 3/7/97.

[3] http://www.cdc.gov/nccdphp/ace/prevalence.htm ACE Study - Prevalence – Adverse Childhood Experiences

[4] Snyder, H.N. (2000). *Sexual assault of young children as reported to law enforcement: Victim, incident, and offender characteristics.* National Center for Juvenile Justice, U.S. Department of Justice.

[5] Simpson, C. Odor, R. & Masho, S. (2004 August). *Childhood Sexual Assault Victimization in Virginia.* Center for Injury & Violence Prevention. Virginia Department of Health.

[6] Snyder, H.N. (2000). *Sexual assault of young children as reported to law enforcement: Victim, incident, and offender*

characteristics. National Center for Juvenile Justice, U.S. Department of Justice.

[7] Ferguson et al, (1996) Childhood sexual abuse and Psychiatric Disorder in Young Adulthood I: Prevalence of sexual abuse and factors associated with sexual abuse. *J Am Acad. Child Adolescent Psychiatry*, 35:1355-1364

Finkelhor, (1993) Epidemiological factors in the clinical identification of child sexual abuse. *Child Abuse and Neglect* 17: 67-70

Sobsey, et al, (1997) Gender differences in abused children with and without disabilities, *Child Abuse and Neglect 21*: 707-720

US Department of Health and Human Services (1998) *Child Maltreatment: 1996: Reports from the States to the National Child Abuse and Neglect Data System.* Washington DC: US Government Printing Office.

[8] Finkelhor, D. (1993) Epidemiological factors in the clinical identification of child sexual abuse. *Child Abuse and Neglect* 17:67-70; *U.S. Department of Health and Human Services,* (1998.)

[9] Finkelhor, 1993

[10] Mullen et al, (1993) Childhood sexual abuse and mental health in adult life. *Br .J. Psychiatry* 163:721- 732.

[11] Fergusson, et al, (1996) Childhood sexual abuse and psychiatric disorder in young adulthood, I: prevalence of sexual abuse and factors associated with sexual abuse. *Journal of American Academy of Child & Adolescent Psychiatry* 35: 1355-1364.

Mullen et al, (1993), Nelson et al, (2002) Association between self-reported childhood sexual abuse and adverse psychosocial outcomes : results from a twin study, *Arch Gen Psychiatry* 59: 139-146.

[12] Abel, G. & Harlow, N. (2001). *Stop child molestation book.* Abel and Harlow.

[13] Kilpatrick, D. Saunders, B., & Smith, D. (2003). Youth victimization: Prevalence and implications. U.S. Department of Justice, National Institute of Justice report.

[14] Snyder, H.N. (2000) *Sexual assault of young children as reported to law enforcement: Victim, incident, and offender characteristics*. National Center for Juvenile Justice, U.S. Department of Justice.

[15] Abel research on National Violence Databank

[16] Abel, G., Becker, J., Mittelman, M., Cunningham-Rathner, J., Rouleau, J., & Murphy, W. (1987) Self reported sex crimes on non-incarcerated paraphiliacs. *Journal of Interpersonal Violence, 2(1)*, 3-25.

[17] Finkelhor, D., & Dziuba-Leatherman, J. (1994). Children as victims of violence: A national survey. *Pediatrics*, 94, 413-420.

[18]Hanson, R. F., Resnick H. S., Saunders, B. E., Kilpatrick, D. G., & Best, C. (1999). Factors related to the reporting of childhood rape. *Child Abuse & Neglect*, 23, 559-69.

[19] U.S. Department of Justice. (2003). Youth Victimization: Prevalence and Implications. Washington, D.C.: National Institute of Justice. (NCJ No. 194972).

[20] Smith, W., Letourneau, E., Saunders, B., Kilpatrick, D, Resnick, H.,& Best, C. (2000). Delay in disclosure of childhood rape: results from a national survey. *Child Abuse & Neglect, Volume 24, Issue 2*, February 2000, Pages 273-287.

[21] Lyon, T.D. (2002). Scientific Support for Expert Testimony on Child Sexual Abuse Accommodation. In J.R. Conte (Ed.), Critical issues in child sexual abuse (pp. 107-138). Newbury Park, CA: Sage.

[22] Hunter, J. A., Goodwin, D. W., & Wilson, R. J. (1992). Attributions of blame in child sexual abuse victims: An analysis of age and gender influences. *Journal of Child Sexual Abuse*, 1, 75-89.

23 Immediate and Long-Term Impacts of Child Sexual Abuse"
by John Briere and Diana Elliott, 1994, *Sexual Abuse of Children,* Vol. 4, Number 2.

24 Gries, L.; Goh, D.; Andrews, M.; Gilbert, J.; Praver, F.;
Stelzer, D. (2000). "Positive reaction to disclosure and
recovery from child sexual abuse". *Journal of Child Sexual Abuse,* 9 (1): 29–51.

25 Kogan, S. (2005). "The Role of Disclosing Child Sexual
Abuse on Adolescent Adjustment and Revictimization".
Journal of Child Sexual Abuse, 14 (2): 25–47.

26 Immediate and Long-Term Impacts of Child Sexual Abuse"
by John Briere and Diana Elliott, 1994, *Sexual Abuse of Children,* Vol. 4, Number 2.

28 Berliner, L. & Elliott, D. (2002). Sexual Abuse of Children,
The APSAC Handbook on Child Maltreatment, Second Edition,
p. 55-78.

29 Berliner, L. & Elliott, D. (2002). Sexual Abuse of Children,
The APSAC Handbook on Child Maltreatment, Second Edition,
p. 55-78.

30 Boyer, Debra, and Fine, David (1992) "Sexual Abuse as a
Factor in Adolescent Pregnancy andChild Maltreatment,"
Family Planning Perspectives.

31 Silbert, M. "Compounding Factors in the Rape of Street
Prostitutes," (1988) Cited in Wolbert-Burgess, A. *Rape and
Sexual Assault II*: Garland Publishing, Inc., New York, p. 77.

32 Marx, B., Heidt, J., & Gold, S. (2005). Perceived
Uncontrollability and Unpredictability, Self-Regulation,
and Sexual Revictimization, *Review of General Psychology,*
Vol.9, 1, 67-90.

33 Marx, B.P., Heidt, J.M. & Gold, S.D. (2005). Perceived
Uncontrollability and Unpredictability, Self-Regulation,
and Sexual Revictimization. *Review of General Psychology,*
Vol. 9, No. 1, 67-90.

[34] Ferguson et al, (1996) Childhood sexual abuse and psychiatric disorder in young adulthood, II: psychiatric outcomes of childhood sexual abuse. *J American Academy of Child – Adolescent Psychiatry 35*: 1365-1374.

Polusny M., Follette, V. (1995) Long term correlates of child sexual abuse: theory and review of the empirical literature. *Applied Prev Psychology 4*: 143-166.

Chapter 5: *Who Are the Sexual Abusers?*

Introduction

For many in this country, the concept of someone who could sexually abuse a child is something too horrible to contemplate. The urge to label sex offenders as "monsters" is a natural one, and there is no question that to commit a sex offense against a child is to commit a terrible crime. Labeling offenders monsters, however, is to place them outside of our experience – to dismiss and, hopefully, banish them to some far off place where they never need trouble us again. The reality, however, is that sex offenders are not monsters. They are fathers, mothers, grandfathers, grandmothers, sons, daughters, aunts, uncles, teachers, coaches, and family friends. The vast majority of sexual offenses against children are committed by someone the child knows and trusts. If anything, this can seem even more frightening than the idea of the offender as monster – the offender could be anyone. This is why it is important for parents to understand as much as they can about how sex offenders of all kinds operate. Such knowledge can help parents recognize trouble, hopefully before any real harm is done. The purpose of this chapter, therefore, is to educate parents about sexual offenders.

This chapter is split into 3 major sections: adult sex offenders, adolescent sex offenders, and children who sexually abuse younger children. The major focus of this chapter is on sexual offenses against children, and thus sex offenses such as peeping, rape, and exposing will not be addressed in great

detail. For suggestions on how to protect your children from
sexual abuse, see Chapter 6.

Adult Sex Offenders

Research has shown time and time again that there is
no such thing as a "typical" child molester, and that there is
no child molester "profile." Profiles can be dangerously
misleading, causing people to discount their suspicions of
someone because that individual does not fit the "profile."
While there is no known profile of a sexual offender, statistics
have been gathered on those who admit having molested a
child. Of the admitted male child molesters[1]:

- 93% considered themselves to be religious

- 77% were married or formerly married

- 79% were Caucasian

- 65% were employed

- 46% were college-educated

In short, the "typical" sex offender looked like an average male. The notion that you can just "tell" who is an offender by looking at them is, unfortunately, a myth.

As we mentioned earlier, most sex offenders have some relationship with the child before molesting the child. This may be because the adult has better access to those children, making it easier to find opportunities to molest them. Having a relationship with the child also makes it easier for the offender to manipulate the child into sexual contact and into not telling anyone about the abuse. For example, an offender may guilt his daughter into the sexual contact by telling her that he feels sad and deprived because her mother won't have sex with him anymore. He may also tell his daughter that if she tells anyone about the abuse then it will result in the family being ripped apart. He could use his ongoing contact with his daughter to repeat this message so she won't tell. Or he could use the ongoing contact to repeatedly threaten her, as many offenders do. We have also seen cases where the offender filmed the sexual abuse and sold the child pornography to others online. In some cases, the offender took "orders" online from customers about the specific sexual acts they wanted to see performed on the victim. The offender then molested the child in that manner and sent the resulting porn to the customer.

Mr. Smith began molesting his daughter, Abby, when she was an infant. He would take her to a hotel and film the abuse there, and then sell the video on the internet. He continued to molest her several times a week and film the abuse. Over time, he became more physically aggressive during the abuse and tied her up with ropes. Despite this, his daughter did not tell anyone about the abuse because he had manipulated her into viewing the sexual activity as his way of treating her as special. He told her that on her 9th birthday, they would celebrate by finally having vaginal intercourse. At the time, she viewed this as a positive event. The 9-year molestation finally ended when a criminal investigator in another country was able to track down the pattern on the hotel bedspread to a small Georgia town. Mr. Smith was arrested and eventually sent to federal prison for producing and trafficking child porn. We should also mention that he was a beloved tennis coach at the local recreation department, and no one, not even his wife, had any clue about his behavior before his arrest.

Types of Child Molesters:

Not all child molesters are the same. You can think of child molesters as falling into two major groups: those who are primarily sexually attracted to children and those who are primarily sexually attracted to adults. Both molest children, but often for different reasons. The first group molests children because they are sexually aroused to children while the second group molests children for a variety of different psychological reasons, such as low self-esteem or poor social skills. The first group has Pedophilia, a serious disorder that involves primary or exclusive sexual interest in children age 13 and younger. Individuals with Pedophilia, called pedophiles, typically molest many more children than child molesters who are not pedophiles. In fact, pedophiles molest 4 times more children than non-pedophile child molesters. On average, pedophiles molest about 11 to 12 children while non-pedophile child molesters molest 2 to 3 children. However, some pedophiles have been known to molest hundreds of victims. Most child molestations are committed by pedophiles, with 95% of child molestations committed by pedophiles, and 88% of child victims molested by pedophiles[2].

Pedophiles start their sexual offending earlier than non-pedophile child molesters, usually when they are adolescents. More than 40% of pedophiles molested a child before age 15, and most pedophiles molested a child before age 20.

Since they usually have little sexual interest in adults, pedophiles are less likely to be married, although some marry in order to give them a veneer of respectability and mask their true intentions. They may also marry to give themselves access to the spouse's children and their friends. Pedophiles may also seek jobs that give them extensive access to children, such as a little league coach or scout troop master. Consider the case of Mr. D:

Mr. D was evaluated after he was arrested for attempting to entice a child. In his interview, Mr. D discussed how he first realized his attraction to young children when he was an adolescent. He committed his first offense when he was 15, molesting a 4-year-old boy in his neighborhood. He was not caught for that offense, and went on to molest 4 more children. In one instance he impersonated a doctor (he was working in a hospital cleaning the linens) and sexually abused a child under the guise of examining him. He was caught for that offense, but instead of being prosecuted he was fired by the hospital; the hospital likely took this course to avoid a public scandal. Mr. D was finally arrested after he approached a boy in his neighborhood and offered to give him a "massage."

Non-pedophile child molesters molest children for a variety of different reasons. Sometimes the molester feels sexually or socially inadequate with adults, and turns to children because he feels more comfortable and in control with them. In other cases the molester develops an unhealthy relationship with one or more of their own children, treating the child more like a spouse than a daughter or son. They eventually progress to molesting the child.

Mr. S was seen for an evaluation and then treatment after he molested his two stepdaughters. Mr. S had been married to the girls' mother for approximately 6 years before he began sexually abusing them. Over the course of treatment, Mr. S indicated that he had become addicted to Internet pornography. His pornography interest contributed to him growing apart from his wife, which in turn led to more extensive pornography use. Mr. S started with more mainstream sites, but as he became bored with them he gravitated toward more deviant sites. He began viewing sites that had themes of bondage, discipline, and rape. Eventually he began viewing sites that dealt with incest. Mr. S then started viewing his stepdaughters in a sexual light, especially after they entered puberty. He began spending more and more time with them, in particular viewing various (non-sexual) Internet sites with each one. He created a situation where it became "normal" for the girls to sit on his lap as they surfed the Internet. He began touching them on their hips before moving on to touching them between their legs and on their breasts. While Mr. S was not sexually attracted to children in general, he developed a very strong sexual attraction to his stepdaughters.

Men Who Molest Boys Versus Girls:

More child molesters molest girls than boys. However, the child molesters who molest boys tend to molest twice as many children. On average, child molesters who molest girls reported having about 5 victims while those who molested boys only reported having about 10 victims. Child molesters who molest both boys and girls had the most victims – 27![3]

It is important to keep in mind that many child molesters molest both girls and boys. Therefore, one should not assume that just because a man gets caught for molesting a girl that he would not also molest a boy, or vice versa. We often see parents make this incorrect assumption when there has been sexual abuse in their family. For example, a mother discovers that her ex-husband has molested her daughter, and she assumes that it is still safe to send her son on visits with the ex-husband. However, the ex-husband may be the type of child molester who molests both girls and boys.

Many people assume that men who molest boys must

be gay. However, over 70% of men who molest boys describe themselves as being heterosexual in their adult sexual preferences[4]. And, most of the men were married or had been married or were living with an adult partner.

Adult Female Offenders:

In studies of adult sex offenders, 1 to 3% of the offenders were female while the rest were male[5]. However, this is thought to be an underestimate of the actual number of female sex offenders, as people often do not view females as sex offenders, even when they commit the same behavior as their male counterparts. Thus, sex offenses by females are often not reported to the authorities. In this author's own research with men in prison for child molestation, she found that many of the men described having childhood experiences where a much older female engaged in sexual behaviors with them. However, the men did not view the sexual activity as abuse. Instead, the men often romanticized the experience as their "initiation" to sex by an older woman, and none of the abuse had been reported to the authorities.

Mary Kay Letourneau is a well-known example of a female sex offender, a former schoolteacher who molested one of her 13-year-old male students. The media often treat sexual offenses involving female offenders as somehow being less serious than offenses perpetrated by male offenders. For example, the Wikipedia entry for Letourneau states, "In 1996 while Letourneau was a Des Moines, Washington elementary school teacher, her *relationship* [emphasis added] with 13-year-old student Vili Fualaau transformed from friendship into flirtation and sex."[6] When was the last time you heard of a male schoolteacher having a "relationship" with a 13-year-old girl? Letourneau later married her victim, and incredibly enough has hosted several parties named "Hot For Teacher" nights, essentially celebrating her molestation – and subtly placing the blame on the boy she molested.[7] This kind of distortion is particularly common in cases where the female offender is relatively young and attractive, and the victim is a teenage boy. In our practice, we have treated female offenders who insist they were somehow "seduced" by their victims, as if your average 14-year-old boy had the sexual magnetism of James Bond.

Regardless of the perceptions generated by the media, sexual offenses by women against young boys are very serious, and just as damaging as offenses by male offenders. As noted above, the victims themselves often have a distorted perception of the offense, viewing it as a "positive" or sexually exciting experience without considering how it may have affected their own sexual development. One male sex offender treated in our program revealed that he had been molested by an older girl when he was a young boy. Even then, in treatment for molesting his daughter, this offender insisted that he had not been harmed in any way by the older girl's actions. Another offender had been molested by his nanny and he later went on to adopt several children and molest them. He romanticized his relationship with his nanny, viewing her as his first true love who taught him about sex. He later used that distorted thinking to justify his own molestation of his children.

Common Myths about Adult Sex Offenders

MYTH: *Child molesters are usually strangers who stalk a child for a period of time, and then abduct them.*

As noted above, the great majority of sexual offenses against children are perpetrated by someone the child knows and trusts. Statistics from Vermont and New Hampshire showed that in 2004, sex crimes were 10 times more likely to be committed by a member of the victim's own family than by a stranger.[8] A 2000 survey by the Bureau of Justice Statistics has shown that only 7% of sexual offenses against a child were committed by a stranger.[9]

Most incidents of child molestation are preceded by a period of time where the perpetrator tries to build a special relationship with the child, a process known in the field as "grooming." The perpetrator may give the child gifts, or allow the child to break a rule to show they aren't like "other" adults. In the Martin Scorsese remake of *Cape Fear*, for example, the Robert de Niro character establishes a bond with the young girl played by Juliette Lewis by allowing her to "catch" him smoking marijuana, and then offering her a chance to smoke it herself. While the movie is fictional, it nonetheless accurately depicts a method used by adult perpetrators to get close to prospective victims. The continued belief that sexual offenders are usually strangers is propagated by the mainstream media, which gives considerable attention to cases of child molestation that involve a stranger (usually someone who has already been convicted of a previous sexual offense) abducting, molesting, and then killing a child. The media pay comparatively little attention to cases of children being molested, say, by family members.[10]

MYTH: *Child molesters commit their offenses because they themselves were molested when they were children*

This myth continues to be expressed with authority by the media. One episode of the popular crime drama *Law and Order: Special Victims Unit* had the so-called psychologist "expert" agree that most sex offenders were molested as children. In fact, extensive research studies have shown that less than half of adult sex offenders were sexually abused when they were children.[11] Even if an offender was molested as a child, that history does not *cause* the offender to then go on and commit a sexual offense. In fact, most sexual abuse victims never molest a child. Instead, the offender makes a *choice* to offend, and being sexually abused is no more an excuse for his behavior than "I was drunk" or "I wasn't thinking." It is important to note that in treatment, an offender's history of sexual victimization is not insignificant and is given considerable attention. The offender would be mistaken, however, to assert that his being molested as a child somehow "made" him go on to molest someone else. Having said that, it does appear that having a history of severe sexual abuse is associated with more severe offending among child molesters. Specifically, child molesters who were sexually abused more than 50 times had over 3 times the number of child victims compared to child molesters who did not have their own history of sexual abuse. Also, 82% of the child molesters who were severely sexually abused were considered to be pedophiles[12].

MYTH: *Child molesters are incapable of change, and treatment does no good.*

In fact, certain forms of treatment have been shown to significantly reduce the probability that an offender will commit another sexual offense. However, the offender must *want* to change in order for treatment to have any chance of success. All too often, the men who go through court-ordered treatment programs in the community are merely there to wait out the clock, do the minimum work required, and get on with their lives. They do not necessarily plan to reoffend, but they are unwilling to make the kinds of serious changes in their lives that are needed to reduce their risk. This may be a somewhat cynical perspective by a treatment provider, but it is born of hard experience in working with these men (and in rarer cases, women). We have treated offenders who genuinely want to change and have been willing to work at it, but in our experience this is sadly the exception rather than the rule.

MYTH: *Homosexuals are more likely to molest children.*

This is not true, as the rates for heterosexuals who molest children are the same as homosexuals who molest children. Therefore, being homosexual or gay does not increase the likelihood that someone will molest a child.

Which Children Do Child Molesters Target?

Ninety percent of child molesters molested a child they already knew, usually someone in their family or within their social circle or neighborhood. In a study of 3,952 child molesters[13]:

- 68% molested a child in their family
- 19% molested their biological child
- 30% molested their stepchild, adopted or foster child
- 18% molested their nieces or nephews
- 5% molested their grandchildren
- 40% molested their friends' children or their neighbors' children

These numbers show that most child molesters molest children in their own families. Men who molest their own children often molest children outside of their family as well. Almost 24% of men who molested their own children also molested the children of their friends or neighbors.

These numbers clearly show that if your child is molested, it is likely that the offender is well known to you and your child, and quite possibly in your family. It is unlikely that your child will be molested by a stranger.

Adolescent Sex Offenders

Adolescent offenders (ages 13 to 17) comprise a disconcertingly large percentage of those who offend against children. A 2009 report by the Department of Justice showed that adolescents were responsible for over a *third* of all sexual offenses against children.[14]

Why Do They Do It?

There are a number of reasons why adolescents commit sexual offenses against children. Here are some examples:

- ◆ Some adolescents have a preferential sexual interest in children. The cause for such a sexual interest is still unclear. Some have argued that there is a biological component to pedophilia, but this has not been conclusively shown. It is important to note that the majority of adolescent offenders are *not* budding pedophiles. Those that are, however, are likely to begin their offending history as adolescents or even younger.

- ◆ Some adolescents have strong feelings of inadequacy around their peers, and believe that they have little to no chance of a sexual relationship with someone close to their own age. They may have had a bad experience in dating a peer, or they may have never tried. Such adolescents often feel more comfortable with younger children because the adolescent is clearly the one in charge. In addition, these adolescents tend to be rather immature, and simply relate better to younger children. These adolescents may then start thinking of the children they have contact with in sexual terms, as a possible outlet for their sexual desires.

♦ Some adolescents have been victims of severe physical abuse and/or neglect. These adolescents have lived a large part of their childhood in a state of helplessness. They crave power and control, and may turn to sexually abusing children as a way to gain that sense of control.

♦ Some adolescents were prematurely sexualized at an early age through sexual abuse, exposure to adult sexual activity, exposure to pornography, or a combination of these factors. These adolescents may have started their offending when they were younger. If they are never caught, or if they were caught but the offense was not properly dealt with (for example brushed off as nothing more than childhood curiosity), they may continue to offend on into adolescence. Their offending, then fueled by the increased sexual drive associated with puberty, may also increase in frequency and intensity.

Should Adolescent Offenders Be Treated Like Adults?

Concerns about adolescent offenders have become so pronounced that many state governments have passed legislation aimed at treating these offenders as if they were adults. While there are some cases where an adolescent offender should be charged as an adult and face adult consequences, most adolescent offenders should *not* be handled as if they were merely younger adults. Research has shown that adolescent offenders are different from adult sex offenders in that they are less likely to reoffend, engage in fewer abusive behaviors over shorter periods of time, and tend to have less aggressive sexual behavior.[15] Adolescent offenders must accept responsibility for their actions and face the consequences for them, including sex offender treatment. However, forcing an adolescent offender to register as a sex offender for a substantial portion of his or her life is often excessive. Harsher penalties for adolescent offenders make it less likely that their parents will cooperate with the authorities and get their child into treatment. In our experience, many parents of adolescent offenders have cooperated with the courts and encouraged their child to plead guilty, with the expectation that the child will receive help. Parents who are faced with their child being labeled a sexual predator and put on an online registry are going to be more willing to challenge the case in court, which in turn causes more strain on juvenile courts and may put victims of the offenses through the strain of testifying. It may also result in the adolescent not being punished or treated for the offending.

Having said that, there are some cases where it is appropriate – and even crucial – to charge the adolescent as an adult. This typically is the case when the adolescent is older, 16 or 17 years old, and the offense is particularly heinous. If a 17-year-old boy commits rape and is sentenced as a juvenile, there is a good chance that he will have completed little, if any, treatment before he turns 18 and his sentence ends. Depending on the state laws, his juvenile record may also be sealed, resulting in him starting over with a "clean slate." Sentencing such an adolescent as an adult is strong medicine, but it at least ensures that he will have to finish his counseling.

Adolescent Female Offenders

As with adult sex offenders, the majority of adolescent sex offenders are male. However, there are a substantial number of adolescent girls who commit sexual offenses. A 2009 report in the *OJJDP Juvenile Justice Bulletin* indicated that juvenile females accounted for 7% of all juvenile arrests for sexual offenses (not counting prostitution).[16] Here are some important facts about female adolescent offenders:

♦ Their average age at the time of the offense is 14.

♦ The victim is typically around 5 years old, and is an acquaintance or relative.

♦ The offenses typically involve fondling, and are part of some kind of caretaking activity – such as babysitting.

♦ Female offenders are more likely to have a history of being physically or sexually abused than male offenders. Those who have a history of being sexually abused are more likely to have been molested by multiple perpetrators, starting at a young age.

Current research suggests that sex offenses by female adolescents are more likely to go unreported, and if they are reported that they are not treated as seriously as offenses committed by male adolescents. One reason may be that many adults, including those in law enforcement and the mental health professions, simply cannot believe that an adolescent female could commit such offenses. Even if they believe that a particular girl committed a sex offense, they may believe that she is unlikely to reoffend. This could be due in part to the commonly held belief that adolescent girls are more mature than adolescent boys, and will more readily grasp the seriousness of the behavior and why it cannot continue. It is very important for parents and authorities to understand that these offenses are very serious, and the girls who commit them are in need of specialized treatment, just like their male counterparts.

Children Who Molest Other Children

Of the three main categories of sexual abusers, the category of children who molest other children is probably the most misunderstood. When parents catch a child sexually abusing another child, the overwhelming temptation is to write off the incident as mere "curiosity" and "exploring." As has been discussed in Chapter 2, however, there is a clear line between healthy, normal sexual behavior in children and sexually abusive behavior. If an older child acts out sexually with a significantly younger child, or if a child uses bribes, tricks, or force to get another child to go along with sexual touching, that is abusive behavior. It is important that such incidents are treated with the seriousness they deserve, because the majority of the time such behavior will not go away on its own.

Who Are These Children?

Among school-aged children with sexual behavior problems, about 33% were girls. However, among preschool aged children with sexual behavior problems, 65% were girls[17]. Boys with sexual behavior problems first molest, on average, when they are about 8 years old while their female counterparts first molest when they are about 6. The most common age of onset for this behavior is between the ages of 6 and 9.

Children with sexual behavior problems may molest just one child or multiple children, and they often target children who are between 4 and 7 years old. They usually target siblings, friends, or acquaintances. The victims are more often female than male.[18] If the offense occurs in the home, the sexually aggressive child often molests the younger, favored child, or biological or stepchild in the family. For example, we see many cases where a teenaged boy's parent remarries, and the boy resents his new younger half-sibling or stepsibling, feeling like that child gets more attention. The teenage boy then molests the younger child.

Were These Children Sexually Abused Themselves?

Many children with sexual behavior problems do have their own history of sexual abuse. However, studies show that 4 to 62% of children with sexual behavior problems have no known history of sexual abuse[19]. Those children may have developed their sexual behavior problems in response to other factors such as exposure to nudity or sexual activity in the home, exposure to sexual materials, physical abuse and/or exposure to domestic violence.[20]

It's important to keep in mind that most sexually abused children do not go on to molest other children. However, there are several factors that appear to increase the chances of a sexually abused child developing a sexual behavior problem. One study[21] outlined four such factors:

- Younger age at time of sexual victimization
- Higher rates of abusive incidents
- Longer period of time between abuse & disclosure
- Lower level of perceived family support following disclosure

Another study examined which sexually abused children went on to molest other children. In an ongoing research study[22] by the Child Molestation Research & Prevention Institute, of 2,811 sexually abused adolescent males, 2,034 went on to molest another child. On average, the boys were about 7 years old when they were sexually abused, and they committed their own sexual offense when they were about 11. The boys who went on to become perpetrators had the following factors in common:

- They were younger than 9 when sexually abused
- They knew nothing about sex before they were sexually abused

- They continued to be upset by the molestation long after it occurred
- They were molested by a person they looked up to
- They became sexually aroused while they were being molested
- They were molested by a boy more than 3 years older than themselves
- They took baths or showers with their sexual abuser
- The abuser put their tongue in the victim's mouth
- The abuser was living in the victim's house
- The victim was molested by more than one person

Sexually abused girls who went on to become perpetrators had the following factors in common:

- They were less than 9 years old when sexually abused.
- They were touched by a woman.
- They sometimes experience flashbacks of their abuse when their girlfriend or boyfriend rubs their chest.
- They sometimes became sexually aroused when being sexually abused.

Since these factors increase a child's risk of molesting others, we recommend that the child address these specific factors in therapy. For example, if a child experienced sexual arousal during his victimization then he should talk about those feelings during his therapy. The therapist could then help the child process his thoughts and feelings about the experience and help him understand that such a reaction is common. We believe that if the child addresses these issues then the child is less likely to develop a sexual behavior problem.

Characteristics of Children Who Molest:

Few Friends

Children who molest tend to have few friends, particularly friends their own age. They often choose to play with much younger children since they have been rejected by children their own age; some have been rejected because they are hyperactive and socially immature. These children may be interested in activities that much younger children like rather than activities shared by their peers. Many children who molest have been diagnosed with Attention-Deficit/Hyperactivity Disorder (ADHD). While some of these children truly have ADHD, others may have been misdiagnosed with ADHD, as they are showing hyperactivity and problems with attention. However, these symptoms can be related to underlying trauma, such as from physical or sexual abuse, rather than an attention disorder.

Another reason that these children may choose to play with much younger children is because they can boss around younger children. Children who molest often have a strong desire to be in control and tell others what to do. Peers often do not allow this, and may end up disliking the child because he or she is too bossy. These bossy children try to control others by insisting that they choose the game they will play, they make the rules, and they tell others what to do. Children who molest may have a strong desire to be in control because they have lacked that control in other areas of their life. For example, they may have felt helpless and out of control when being abused or when having witnessed abuse or domestic violence. They may then try to regain control by controlling others. Children who molest may also choose to play with younger children so they can have the opportunity to molest younger children. One of the easiest ways for older children to molest younger children is to gain their trust through play and then molest them during the play. For example, the older child may initiate a game of "doctor," "house," or Truth or Dare and then molest the other child in the course of the game. This can be confusing to the victimized child who may not recognize that the sexual activity is inappropriate and may assume that the touching is just a normal part of the game.

Low Frustration Tolerance

Children who molest tend to have a low frustration tolerance, often getting angry when things do not go their way. As noted above, they also tend to have a strong need for control. They frequently engage in aggressive behavior, and have poor problem-solving skills. Because of their aggressive and angry behavior, they may be diagnosed with Conduct Disorder or Oppositional Defiant Disorder. (Children cannot be diagnosed with both Conduct Disorder *and* Oppositional Defiant Disorder; Oppositional Defiant Disorder can only be diagnosed if the child does not meet the criteria for Conduct Disorder). As the name suggests, Oppositional Defiant Disorder involves a pattern of oppositional and defiant behavior while Conduct Disorder involves more serious behavioral problems such as fire-setting, stealing, animal cruelty, truancy, and running away. For children who have these disorders, sexually aggressive behavior may be just one other type of behavioral problem that they display.

Dysfunctional Home Life

Children who molest other children usually come from dysfunctional homes where they have experienced some type of abuse or neglect. Many of these children were physically or sexually abused, exposed to domestic violence, and/or exposed to adult sexual activity or sexually explicit materials. These children often have a history of long-standing problems with their parents. Many of their parents have their own childhood history of abuse, as well as a history of substance abuse as adults. These parents also tend to have significant psychological problems and personality disorders. About half of these children come from single parent homes.

Why Do These Children Act Out Sexually?

There is no single reason why some children act out sexually. Instead, there can be many different reasons for this behavior:

- Some children act out sexually because they are repeating sexual behaviors that they have seen, either in real life, in magazines, or on TV/videos. Some children are curious about what they have seen and they want to try these things that they have seen adults do. This is just like children repeating other behaviors that they witness, such as a toddler pretending to be a mother to its baby doll, imitating her own mother's actions.

- Some children like the "high" of doing something they know they are not supposed to do, such as sexual behaviors. These children have been exposed to sexual behavior in some way and they want to do sexual things because it is forbidden. They may think that they should be able to do whatever their older siblings or parents are doing. They may also want to be "cool" and may think that this is what cool kids do. They may have overheard other children talking about sexual things, which made them feel like they needed to do the same.

- Some children act out sexually as a way to distract from negative feelings they cannot handle, such as anxiety, anger, sadness, etc. You can think of the sexual acting out as just another way for the child to act out. For example, some children act out by throwing tantrums, hitting others, and cursing, while others act out by doing sexual things. However, the child must have somehow learned this sexual behavior, which could be from seeing sexual activity or pornography, or having been sexually abused.

• Some children were sexually abused and are repeating these same sexual behaviors with other children. They may repeat the behaviors because they experienced positive feelings and/or sexual arousal during their own sexual victimization. It can be hard to imagine that a child may have any positive feelings or sexual arousal during victimization; however, the sexual touching of a child's genitals can feel good to the child, just as an adult's genitals react when touched. This is a normal bodily reaction to the touching of genitals. This can be a very confusing experience for the child, as the child may also be feeling sad or scared at the same time they are experiencing a positive physical sensation. Children who experience positive physical sensations often feel very guilty and ashamed, and may come to believe that they somehow asked for or wanted the abuse since their body reacted to the touching. This guilt can be further compounded by the perpetrator saying things to the child such as, "you know you want it." Perpetrators often say such things to their victims to make themselves feel less guilty and less responsible for their abusive behavior. They also tend to say such things to make the child feel guilty and responsible for the abuse so the child will be less likely to tell anyone about the abuse.

Children who were sexually abused may also repeat the sexual behaviors because this is how they have learned to relate to other people. For example, it is common for boys who have been molested by their mothers to show sexualized behaviors toward other adult women. They may have learned that this is what adult women expect or want from them. Thus, they may simply repeat the behaviors that they were taught, such as rubbing their mothers' breasts or caressing her hair. Consider the case of Keisha:

Keisha was sexually abused on a daily basis by her father from ages 2 to 7. Her father fondled her vagina and performed oral sex on her. Keisha thought that this was normal for a father to do to his daughter. She was upset and did not understand when she was taken into foster care. She said that the sexual touching felt good and she wanted to return home so her father could touch her again. She was masturbating compulsively to the point of rubbing her genitals raw, and said she wanted her father to lick and touch her "private" because it hurt her hand to continually rub herself. While in foster care, she fondled a 5-year-old girl and sexually propositioned her foster father. She did not understand when her foster father told her this was inappropriate. Keisha attended therapy for two years and was able to stop her compulsive masturbation and stop touching other children. She grew to understand why her father's behavior was wrong. She later testified at his criminal trial and he was sent to prison. Fortunately, she was adopted by a family and went on to make straight A's, become a cheerleader, and was well-liked among her peers.

Children who were sexually abused may act out sexually when they feel angry, as they have learned to associate anger with sex. For example, a girl who is molested whenever her stepfather is angry may learn that you do sexual things to people when you are mad. Other sexually abused children may act out sexually when angry because that is just another way to act out anger. Here is the case of Brian:

Brian is a 9-year-old boy who stuck his finger in his 3-year-old foster brother's anus following a court hearing involving his parents. Brian had been angry that day because his father had refused to hug him when he saw him at court. Brian had been removed from his parents' care by the state due to physical abuse. After Brian was removed from the home, he disclosed that he had been sexually abused by his father and older brother. Brian was later caught having his 5-year-old brother perform oral sex on him in the bathroom at summer camp. Brian also acted out his anger by urinating all over his foster parents' furniture while they were asleep at night. In addition, he had thoughts of killing himself. Brian's behavioral problems were so severe that he ended up being placed in a secure residential treatment facility. He is a good example of how sexual abuse can damage a child and result in the child having numerous emotional, behavioral, and sexual problems.

- Some children may do sexual things because they like the way their body feels when their genitals are touched. They may have accidentally discovered this on their own or during sexual exploration with peers. They may have also experienced sexual arousal when witnessing sexual activity or during sexual abuse by an older person.

Rick is a 9-year-old boy who has been in and out of a string of residential treatment centers and psychiatric hospitals due to his sexual acting out. His sexual problems began at age 5 when a fellow classmate in his Kindergarten class performed oral sex on him in the bathroom. Rick then began to act out sexually with other children his age. When reprimanded for his behavior, Rick then turned to his three younger siblings, as he thought he could trick them into sexual activity and intimidate them into not telling their parents. However, his younger brother eventually told on him. Rick was then removed from his home and was placed in residential treatment, but he continued to act out sexually, this time with the other children in the treatment program. He eventually ended up in a locked psychiatric hospital, but continued to engage in fondling and oral sex with other children. When interviewed at age 9, he stated that he likes to trick other children into sexual activity and he specifically targets younger children or those who he thinks he can manipulate. He bribes the children by offering them toys and promising to be their friend if they do sexual things with him. He understands that his behavior is wrong, but admits he has no motivation to stop the behavior because it feels good to him. Rick is a good example of a child who acts out sexually because he likes the physical sensations from the sexual acts.

- While most children know that it is wrong to make others engage in sexual behaviors, some children may not realize that such behavior is wrong. These children may live in a home where they see a lot of sexual activity or sexual material, or they have been sexually abused, such that they think that it is normal to make others do sexual things.

How Do These Children Feel About Their Behavior?

During the molestation, children who molest often feel happy and in control. Afterwards, however, they often worry that they will get in trouble. Sometimes they get so worried that they seek relief from feeling bad, so they act out sexually again. The child often feels a "tug-of-war" in their conscience about what they are doing. However, their guilt is usually temporary and does not result in them permanently stopping the behavior. Instead, it usually requires them getting caught before they change their behavior. For some children, the shame of getting caught may be enough to prevent them from acting out sexually again. However, for other children, their sexual problems will continue without treatment.

What Do These Children Do When Confronted?

Unfortunately, most children who molest deny their sexual acting out, even when caught in the act. In one survey, only 10.3% of the children assumed responsibility for their sexually aggressive behaviors. These children seem to show the same strong denial that teens and adults show when confronted about their sexual offending. It seems that even young children are aware that they are not supposed to act out sexually, so they deny their behavior in the hope that they will not get in trouble. Many times, adults mistakenly assume that the child's emotional and intense denial means that the child is telling the truth. For example, we have had many parents tell us that their child must not have acted out sexually as accused because the child started to cry and loudly protested that he/she did not do this. Unfortunately, the child's strong emotional reaction only tells us that the child is very upset about being accused of such, not that the child is innocent of the accusations. These children often show such a strong reaction because they are intensely afraid of getting in trouble, as they know they have done something wrong. They think that if they just say they didn't do it, the adults will drop it and it will all go away. Sometimes, the children have learned this from seeing others deny their misbehavior. For example, children who have been sexually abused often see their own perpetrators flatly deny their molesting behaviors, so the child has learned that you simply deny your behavior to avoid punishment.

If and when children admit to their sexual acting out, they often do not tell the whole truth about their behavior. Instead, they often falsely claim that the other child started the sexual behaviors, agreed to the sexual behaviors, and/or wanted them to continue. It usually turns out that this is not the case, and that the sexually aggressive child just wants to shift blame and responsibility away from himself. Consider the case of Josh:

> *9-year-old Josh was caught acting out sexually with Sam, the 4-year-old son of his father's girlfriend. When asked about his behavior, Josh indicated that Sam had touched his penis with his hand and mouth, claiming that Sam had started the behavior. He said, "Sam just started doing it and he made me start doing it." Josh stated that Sam called it the "mommy and daddy game." Josh portrayed himself as being unable to resist pressure from 4-year-old Sam to play this game. When asked to explain what happened, Josh said, "First he was getting on top of me." When asked what happened next, Josh stated that he pushed Sam off of him, but he "kept on doing it." Josh indicated that he was wearing his pajamas and then Sam "started doing it." He reported that his pants were down when Sam got on top of him. He initially reported that Sam was responsible for taking his pants down; however, he later admitted that he had taken his own pants down. When asked if any of the touching was his fault, Josh said that he was only at fault for "going along with it."*

Josh's case is a perfect example of how children who molest often portray the younger child as initiating the sexual behavior and even pushing them into it. While Josh's parents might want to believe Josh's story, they should not, as it is extremely unlikely that any 4-year-old could pressure a 9-year-old child into sexual behavior against his will. The 9-year-old child is physically much larger, more emotionally sophisticated, and likely to be in control, given his age. The only way that the 4-year-old could be in control is if the 9-year-old was severely mentally retarded and/or physically disabled. And this is usually not the case.

Children who molest often admit to only part of the sexual behaviors in which they engaged. As in the case above, Josh was accused of putting his finger in Sam's anus as well as performing oral sex on Sam. While Josh admitted to Sam touching his penis with his hand and mouth, Josh denied that he himself did anything sexual to Sam. Thus, he can portray Sam as the aggressor while portraying himself as the victim. This is very common for perpetrators of all ages to admit to only some of the more mild sexual behaviors, particularly those that do not make them look as bad. Unfortunately, parents of sexually aggressive children often want to believe that their child is telling the entire truth because it is easier to believe the child's sanitized version than the victim's version. Many parents justify their belief by telling themselves that their child must be telling the truth since he admitted to some sexual behaviors. However, sexually aggressive children, just like juvenile and adult sex offenders, rarely admit to all of their sexual acting out without first receiving specialized treatment. Even with specialized treatment, it often takes a long time for the sexual abuser to admit to all of the details of their sexual acting out.

The good news is that treatment can help children learn to stop their inappropriate sexual behaviors. In one study, most of the children showed significantly fewer sexual behavior problems after outpatient treatment that lasted 12 to 32 weeks.[23] Other research shows that with appropriate treatment, most children with sexual behavior problems will not commit a sex offense as an adult. One study found that 10 years after receiving treatment, 98% of these children had not committed a sex offense[24].

What are Signs of Someone Who Could Pose a Sexual Risk to My Child?

An adult or older child who:

Tries to gain access to children

- Chooses to spend most of his free time around younger children rather than around peers
- Often tries to be alone with children
- Often offers to babysit children for free

Displays poor boundaries with children

- Violates children's boundaries by walking in on them when they are undressing or in the bathroom
- Makes sexual comments about children's bodies or physical development
- Shows physical affection to children even though the child does not want it, such as:
  - Kissing
  - Tickling
  - Wrestling
- Leaves pornography in areas of the home where the children could see it, such as on the bathroom floor
- Leaves pornography on the computer screen
- Leaves door open when showering, masturbating or engaging in sexual activity, when a child is in the home

Treats children in an unusually special manner

- Often buys gifts for a child or gives him money when there is no special occasion
- Treats a child as a peer or friend rather than as a child
- Shows the child special attention

- Often goes beyond the normal or expected role with the child, such as a coach who spends extra time with the child outside of coaching
- Allows or encourages a child to do things that other adults would not typically allow him to do such as drink alcohol, use drugs, or watch R-rated movies or porn

Has *ever* been accused of any type of sex offense

- Child sexual abuse
- Exposing
- Peeping
- Viewing child pornography

Conclusion

This chapter has shown how individuals of all ages, even young children, can engage in abusive sexual behaviors. While parents should not be dismissive of dangers posed by total strangers, it is important to understand that in most cases the sexual abuser has some sort of relationship with the victim that existed for some time before the offense took place. It can be difficult for parents to sense danger, because so many abusers "look" perfectly normal. The next chapter provides information on how parents can protect their children from abusers.

---

[1] Abel, G.G. & Harlow, N. (2001). The Stop Child Molestation Book.
[2] Abel, G.G. & Harlow, N. (2001). The Stop Child Molestation Book.

3 Abel, G.G. & Harlow, N. (2001). The Stop Child Molestation Book.
4 Abel, G.G. & Harlow, N. (2001). The Stop Child Molestation Book.
5 Abel, G.G. & Harlow, N. (2001). The Stop Child Molestation Book.
6 Wikipedia entry, *Mary Kay Letourneau,* http://en.wikipedia.org/wiki/Mary_Kay_Letourneau (retrieved February 2011)
7 ibid
8 Fountain, K. (2006). By the numbers: A statistical portrait of sex offenders. *Valley News,* A7.
9 U.S. Bureau of Justice Statistics. *2000 Sexual Assault of Young Children as Reported to Law Enforcement.* 2000.
10 Cheit, Ross E. (2003). What hysteria? A systematic study of newspaper coverage of accused child molesters. *Child Abuse & Neglect.* 27:607-623.
11 Center for Sex Offender Management (2000). *Myths and Facts About Sex Offenders.* http://www.csom.org/pubs/mythsfacts.html (retrieved February 2011).
12 Abel, G.G. & Harlow, N. (2001). The Stop Child Molestation Book.
13 Abel, G.G. & Harlow, N. (2001). The Stop Child Molestation Book.
14 Office of Juvenile Justice and Delinquency Prevention (2009), *Juvenile Justice Bulletin.*
15 National Center on Sexual Behavior in Youth (2003), Adolescent Sex Offenders: Common Misconceptions versus Current Evidence, *NCSBY Fact Sheet Number 3.*
16 Office of Juvenile Justice and Delinquency Prevention (2009), *Juvenile Justice Bulletin.*

[17] Bonner, B. L., Walker, C. E., & Berliner, L. (1999). Children with sexual behavior problems: Assessment and treatment (Final Report, Grant No. 90-CA-1469). Washington, DC: Administration of Children, Youth, and Families, Department of Health and Human Services. Retrieved from http://www.calib.com/nccanch/pubs/otherpubs/childassessment/index.cfm

Gray, A. S., Pithers, W. D., Busconi, A., & Houchens, P. (1999). Developmental and etiological characteristics of children with sexual behavior problems: Treatment implications. Child Abuse & Neglect, 23, 601-621.

Silovsky, J. F., & Niec, L. (2002). Characteristics of young children with sexual behavior problems: A pilot study. Child Maltreatment, 7, 187-197.

[18] Johnson, T. C. (1988). Child perpetrators: Children who molest other children: preliminary findings. *Child Abuse & Neglect*, 12, 219-229.
Johnson, T. C. (1989). Female child perpetrators: Children who molest other children. *Child Abuse & Neglect*, 13(4), 571-585.

Friedrich, W. N., & Luecke,W.J. (1988). Young school-age sexually aggressive children. Professional Psychology: Research and Practice, 19, 155-164.

[19] Bonner, B. L., Walker, C. E., & Berliner, L. (1999). Children with sexual behavior problems: Assessment and treatment (Final Report, Grant No. 90-CA-1469). Washington, DC: Administration of Children, Youth, and Families, Department of Health and Human Services. Retrieved from http://www.calib.com/nccanch/pubs/otherpubs/childassessment/index.cfm

Gray, A. S., Pithers, W. D., Busconi, A., & Houchens, P. (1999). Developmental and etiological characteristics of children with sexual behavior problems: Treatment implications. Child Abuse & Neglect, 23, 601-621.

Silovsky, J. F., & Niec, L. (2002). Characteristics of young children with sexual behavior problems: A pilot study. Child Maltreatment, 7, 187-197.

[20] Friedrich, W.N. (2002). Psychological assessment of sexually abused children and their families. Thousand Oaks, CA: Sage.

Pithers, W. D., Gray, A., Busconi, A., & Houchens, P. (1998). Children with sexual behavior problems: Identification of five distinct child types and related treatment considerations. Child Maltreatment, 3, 384-406.

[21] Becker, J.V. & Hunter, J.A. (1997). Understanding and treating child and adolescent sexual offenders. *Advances in Clinical Child Psychology*, 19, 177-196

[22] Kirn, T.F. (2006). Survey eyes cycle of sexual abusers and victims. *Clinical Psychiatry News, June.* http://findarticles.com/p/articles/mi_hb4345/is_6_34/ai_n29 281352/ (retrieved February 2011).

[23] Bonner, B. L., Walker, C. E., & Berliner, L. (1999). Children with sexual behavior problems: Assessment and treatment (Final Report, Grant No. 90-CA-1469). Washington, DC: Administration of Children, Youth, and Families, Department of Health and Human Services. Retrieved from http://www.calib.com/nccanch/pubs/otherpubs/childasse ssment/index.cfm

Pithers, W. D., Gray, A., Busconi, A., & Houchens, P. (1998). Children with sexual behavior problems: Identification of five distinct child types and related treatment considerations. Child Maltreatment, 3, 384-406.

[24] Carpentier, M. Y., Silovsky, J. F., & Chaffin, M. (2006). Randomized trial of treatment for children with sexual

behavior problems: Ten-year follow-up. *Journal of Consulting and Clinical Psychology, 74* (3), 482-488.

Chapter 6: How to Protect Your Child From Sexual Abuse

Introduction

No parent wants their child to be sexually abused, but most parents don't know what specific steps they need to take in order to protect their children. Fortunately, there is a lot that parents can do to protect their children. Protecting your children from sexual abuse involves two main components. The first has to do with the child's environment – both in terms of *where* the child is and *who* the child is with. The second has to do with the children themselves.

Obviously, it is impossible and unreasonable to expect any parent to watch their child 24 hours a day, 7 days a week. If a parent actually kept track of the amount of time they spent with their eyes on their child, it would probably amount to a small fraction of the day. This is less the case with infants, but becomes more and more the case as the child grows up. Children naturally want to get out and explore their environment, and as they get older they want increased freedom. How, then, can a parent adequately protect their child from potential dangers? The truth is that it is impossible to foresee every single problem and source of harm that may befall a child. This does *not* mean, however, that a parent should simply give up and leave things to fate. Parents can make a huge difference by casting a critical eye towards those people and places their child will interact with, and making sure that the environment their child is in meets a certain standard of safety.

"Protective Parenting"

There will undoubtedly be criticism by some that our suggestions for parents essentially tell them to assume that danger lies everywhere, and that anyone their child comes in contact with is a potential sex offender. We view our recommendations more along the lines of having a healthy skepticism about people and places. Remember when you learned how to drive? You were taught "defensive driving," which means that you can't assume that other drivers will look out for your best interests. You have to drive with the understanding that other cars represent potential dangers. Your awareness of those dangers is your best defense against them. You can view parenting the same way. The more aware you are of potential dangers, the better you will be able to deal with them. Many cases of sexual abuse occur in part because parents simply assume their child will be safe in a particular place, or with a particular person. Being appropriately skeptical means you can look at a situation objectively, and ask the right questions to determine if it is appropriate for your child.

Part 1: Child's Environment

80% of sexual abuse cases occur when a child is alone with an adult[1]. Given this, you can significantly reduce your child's risk of being molested by reducing the amount of time your child spends alone with an adult. We recommend that whenever you can, choose group situations rather than situations where your child is alone with an adult. You can also choose organizations whose youth activities do not involve a child being alone with an adult. For those activities that do involve such contact, make sure that the organization runs criminal background checks and requires professional references for the adults who work with children.

If your child is alone with an adult, you can reduce the risk of sexual abuse by having this contact occur in a public setting where others can observe their interactions. You can also tell the adult that you will stop by periodically, at different times, which lets the adult know that their time with the child is not completely private. You should also follow through on this by stopping in periodically. In addition, you can give your child a cell phone and tell your child to call you if needed. Also, you should periodically check in with your child before and after their time spent alone with an adult. For example, you could say to your child before the contact, "You are meeting with your tutor this afternoon. How are you feeling about that?" After the contact, you could ask your child, "How did it go with Mike today?" Look to see if your child shows any negative feelings after the contact, and if so, ask your child about this.

When to be Wary of Adults

As we outlined in the previous chapter, most adult sex offenders try to build a "special" relationship with their intended victim before they attempt any sexual contact. This period of time is used by the offender to "groom" the child, to work out a method of being alone with the child, and to psych themselves up to take the final step and commit the offense (for example, offenders who try to blame their offending on alcohol may have in fact become intoxicated to lower their anxiety level and provide so-called "liquid courage" to attempt the offense). There are warning signs parents can look out for that can tip them off that something is wrong.

First, be wary of adults, particularly single adults or male adults, who appear very invested in spending time with your child. In one case a mother became suspicious because the father of her son's friend continually pestered her about having her son come to his house. She was suspicious because even though her son's friend was a teenager and was perfectly capable of expressing himself, it was his father who continually asked for her son to come over. She got the distinct impression that it was much more important to the father than the son that her child go to his house. As it turned out, she was right. The father was asking her son to come over so he could molest him.

Also watch for situations where an adult spends an inordinate amount of time alone with your child. For some busy parents, a friendly neighbor who is happy to spend time with their child, look after them, and take them on trips can seem like a Godsend. There may be a darker reason for their interest, however. One convicted sex offender recalled that one day a mother of a boy he had let stay at his house had come up to him and thanked him for being so willing to spend time with her son. The offender had in fact used that "sleepover" as an opportunity to molest the boy.

In general, parents should be very careful about leaving their children alone with someone they do not know very well. Mothers in particular should avoid leaving their children alone with their new boyfriend whenever possible. We have seen many cases of mothers who worked nights and arranged for their new boyfriend to take care of the children on a regular basis, only to later discover that the boyfriend had been molesting the children while she was at work. These mothers often did not know much about their boyfriend's past before allowing him to assume the primary caretaker role to their children. Unfortunately, child molesters often seek women who have children and who need childcare, as this provides them with easy access to potential victims. In cases where a child was sexually abused in the past, the mother needs to be even more careful, as that child is at increased risk for being sexually abused again. We have seen cases where a mother's boyfriend or husband molested her daughter, and yet the mother the. allowed the next boyfriend to babysit her daughter, resulting in the child being molested by another person.

Parents should also look out for adults who offer to go beyond their normal roles in your child's life, such as a coach who offers to drive your child home. We worked on a case of a high school teacher who offered to take his male students out for dinner and on camping trips. It was later discovered that he was giving the boys alcohol and marijuana, showing them pornographic videos, and then molesting them when they were drunk, high, or passed out. Obviously, the boys' parents were not aware of what was occurring on the outings, but they did know that this teacher was going well beyond his role as a teacher, which should have been a red flag. Here is another case of abuse by a man who used his position to gain the parents' trust:

> *15-year-old Carly was a responsible, straight-A student from an upstanding middle-class family. Carly's parents never thought she would be vulnerable to sexual advances from an adult, and never thought she would hide such behavior from them. However, Carly's gymnastics coach was able to skillfully manipulate her into what she thought was a consensual sexual relationship with him. After having coached Carly for over a year, he slowly broke down the barriers between them by arranging for her to coach a younger girls' team with him. They began spending many hours together at the gym and he began treating her as more of a friend than his student. He then started texting her outside of their gymnastics activities and convinced her to come to his house for dinner. He told her that they couldn't tell anyone or they would both get in trouble. He later convinced her to spend the night with him and he manipulated her into having sex. Carly's parents discovered the molestation when they were talking to Carly's friend who accidentally revealed that Carly had not spent the night at her house as Carly had claimed. The parents wondered how they could have seen this coming.*

One red flag in this case is the sheer number of hours this girl was spending with this coach at the gym, which she estimated to be about 4 hours a day, 7 days a week. The second red flag is the texting between Carly and her coach. If her parents had checked her cell phone they would have quickly realized that this was not a normal student-coach relationship. Fortunately, the parents did discover the molestation when they learned of their daughter's lying. However, this discovery was accidental. This case illustrates the need for parents to know where their children are, even if they are teens, and to verify that this is actually the case, and to know who their children are communicating with via text or the Internet.

Parents should also closely monitor their children around anyone who has been accused of exposing themselves or peeping in windows. The reason is that this behavior may be a sign of a larger sexual problem that could include molesting children. Over 60% of pedophiles engage in other deviant sexual behavior such as exposing and peeping[2].

When to be Wary of Teenagers

When it comes to adolescent sex offenders, many of the warning signs for adults also apply. Keep in mind that most teenagers are not enthused at the prospect of playing with children significantly younger than themselves. They often view it as a chore, something to be endured rather than enjoyed. If you have a teenager – especially a teenage boy – who seeks extensive contact with younger children, treat that teenager cautiously.

Below is an example of a case where a teen molested much younger children. This is a typical case in that the molestation occurred during babysitting, and the parents were shocked when the abuse was discovered:

Johnny is a 16-year-old boy whose parents were friends with a neighborhood couple who had 3 younger boys. Johnny volunteered to babysit for the boys whenever their parents wanted to go out, and asked for relatively little money in return. The parents trusted Johnny because on the surface he was a neatly dressed, well-behaved teenager who earned good grades in school. Over the course of a year, Johnny sexually abused each of the 3 boys. He began by talking to them about sex, and asking them not to tell their parents about it. When the boys kept the secret, Johnny moved on to fondling them and having them perform oral sex on him. He was finally caught when one of the boys accidentally told their mother about a "game" Johnny played with them that involved taking their clothes off. The boys' parents were stunned that a boy like Johnny – who seemed so "nice" – could do such things.

Many parents who would normally not allow a teenage boy to play with their young children make exceptions in the case of teenagers who have developmental disabilities. It seems more "normal" for a developmentally disabled teenager to want to play with younger children, because mentally they often seem much younger themselves. Parents should remember, however, that even though such teenagers may seem "young" mentally, from a physical standpoint they are still much older – they are bigger and stronger than most young children, and once they hit puberty they have the same sexual drives as an average teenager. Consider the case of Harold:

Harold is a 17-year-old boy with mild mental retardation. Harold was often picked on by children his own age so he gravitated towards the younger children in the neighborhood. He also felt more comfortable around younger children. He would play with the younger children in and around the neighborhood's houses, typically without any adult supervision. Because Harold behaved as if he were a younger child, the parents of the other children tended to think of him as being younger. At home, Harold began viewing pornographic sites on the Internet, and often fantasized about having sex. One day he was playing Hide-and-Seek with the neighborhood children, and persuaded a 10-year-old girl to "hide" with him. He then tried to get her to touch his penis. The girl ran away and told. Her parents agreed not to prosecute him if he got into treatment.

We have seen many cases like this, where teens with developmental disabilities were not prosecuted when they committed a sex offense. On the one hand, the lack of prosecution is understandable since the teen has significant intellectual limitations. However, the lack of prosecution often means that the teen never receives appropriate treatment for his sexual problems and he learns that there is no real punishment for his offending. Not surprisingly, this increases his risk for reoffending. Consistent with this, we have seen many of these individuals who continue to molest children and are never held accountable for their behavior.

Potential Places for Child-on-Child Sexual Abuse

In general, the most likely places for child-on-child sexual abuse are settings where older children mix with much younger children, and there is minimal adult supervision. Such settings allow older children who have sexual issues to act out sexually with the younger children. Unfortunately, such sexual acting out can occur even when there is adult supervision, as there are very few situations in which an adult can be watching every child all of the time. Children who act out sexually can do so within a few seconds. For example, an older child can whisper sexual things into a younger child's ear or touch the child's genitals when the teacher looks away. This makes it very challenging to protect your children, and makes it all the more important that you be careful of the environments your children are in.

Based on our clinical experience, here are some of the most common places for child-on-child sexual abuse:

At Daycare

We have seen many cases of sexual abuse in daycares, particularly in settings where older children are allowed to interact freely with much younger children, and there is not enough adult supervision. In some settings, the older children are encouraged to assume a caretaker role to the younger children, such as changing their diapers and taking them to the bathroom. This allows the older child to engage in sexual acts with the much younger child and disguise their sexual behaviors as caretaking. For example, the older child may sexually touch the younger child's vagina while changing the child's diaper or helping the child wipe after using the bathroom. Sexual acting out at daycares often occurs in the bathrooms and during less supervised parts of the day, such as on field trips. Consider the case of Tommy:

Tommy is a 9-year-old boy who repeatedly engaged in inappropriate sexual behavior with younger children at his daycare. He fondled the penis of a 5-year-old boy many times, beneath his underwear, while they were sitting in the back of the bus going on field trips. He also made the 5-year-old fondle his penis. Tommy also pulled down the pants and underwear of several other young boys. On another occasion, he made sexual comments to a younger girl. He continued to act out sexually despite the daycare staff being aware of his sexual issues, trying to separate him from younger children, and his being in specialized treatment for sexual issues. The problem is that there was simply not enough staff to provide the level of supervision needed. Tommy was eventually kicked out of the daycare due to his behaviors.

While in the above example the daycare did eventually kick Tommy out of the daycare, many daycares are reluctant to kick out such children, as they may not want to anger the parent or lose the tuition money. Children who act out sexually should ideally not be in settings with much younger children. However, they often are, due to lack of other practical childcare options. And daycares often try to hide sexual acting out that occurs in their center, for fear of parents withdrawing their children and possibly being sued. In fact, we recently had a case where a daycare was sued by a parent whose 5-year-old daughter was molested by a 5-year-old boy at the daycare. The daycare had been aware of the boy's prior history of sexual acting out, but they allowed him to remain at the daycare. In the end, the daycare agreed to a healthy settlement in order to avoid the cost and media coverage involved in a trial.

Here is another case we had that involved a daycare:

3-year-old Tonya told her mother one day that she did not want to go to daycare anymore. When asked why not, Tonya said that three other children at the daycare had been touching and licking her "toot-toot." Tonya's mother also recalled that, before Tonya made this disclosure, Tonya had been holding her genital area and complaining that it hurt. When Tonya's mother talked to Tonya's daycare teacher, she discovered that the teacher had been aware of several reports of sexual behavior among the children, but the daycare director had instructed her to not tell the parents about it. The teacher then told Tonya's mother that she once caught a 4-year-old boy laying on top of Tonya and humping her. She also said that one of the 4-year-old girls once came into the classroom, dropped her pants, spread her legs, and said, "Kiss my pussy." After talking with the teacher, Tonya's mother told the children in the daycare that they were not supposed to be touching each other's private parts. After Tonya's mother left, one of the boys told Tonya that he would kill her parents because she had told about the touching. Tonya's mother then withdrew Tonya from the daycare. Even after she was removed from the daycare, Tonya continued to show sexual behaviors at home including fondling her vagina in front of others, trying to insert toys in her vagina, touching her mother's breasts, trying to French-kiss others, and trying to get her dog to lick her vagina.

In addition to regular daycares, we have seen numerous cases of children molested by older children at church daycares. In these cases, the abuse was often committed by an older teen who was acting as a helper in the daycare room. Informal daycares at churches often rely on volunteers to provide the childcare, and sexual abusers often seek out these volunteer opportunities. Plus, church settings, almost by definition, tend to be accepting and trusting of others, and may therefore take relatively few precautions to decrease the opportunity for abuse to occur. For example, the volunteers may be allowed to take an individual child to the bathroom, thereby giving the volunteer the chance to molest the child in the stall. Also, the volunteers do not have to undergo the same accreditation process as licensed daycares. Thus, they are not required to check criminal backgrounds as a licensed daycare would.

What Can You Do?

Of course not all daycares have these problems. And we are not advocating for parents to avoid sending their children to daycare. What we do recommend is that parents be careful in choosing their child's daycare center so they can minimize the risk of their child being molested. Ideally, it is best to choose a daycare that:

- Is licensed by the state as a childcare facility
- Is Accredited by the National Association for the Education of Young Children
- Conducts criminal background checks of the staff
- Has a low teacher-to-student ratio
- Provides close adult supervision
- Does not mix children who are 3 or more years apart in age
- Does not have older children in caretaking roles to younger children, particularly with regards to toileting
- Provides close adult supervision when children are in the bathroom with other children
- Provides close adult supervision when children are on field trips and on buses
- Does not allow children to play in areas where they cannot be seen at all times such as in tents or playhouses

In School Bathrooms

Many parents assume that their children are safe at school. Unfortunately, this is sometimes not the case, as we have seen numerous cases of children having been molested by other children at school. One of the most common places for sexual abuse to occur at school is in the bathroom, which is not surprising given that it is a semi-private place that is usually free of adult supervision. It is also a place where older children can gain access to younger children, particularly in elementary school where the ages can range from 5 to 11.

Joe is an 8-year-old boy who suddenly began defecating on himself at home and school. A few months later, he was caught with two 6-year-old boys with their pants down. When questioned about their behavior, the boys told their mother that they had been rubbing each other's private parts. Joe then disclosed to his mother that he had been sexually abused by two older boys in his school bathroom. Specifically, he indicated that these two boys had performed anal sex on him and threatened to kill him if he told anyone. A medical exam showed evidence of tearing in his rectum.

Max is another boy who was sexually abused at school. He was 7 at the time. He began smearing feces on the bathroom wall at home. He also started wetting his pants during the day and night, and showing fear of going to the bathroom alone. In addition, he attempted to have his 3-year-old brother touch his penis and played with his dog's and cat's genitals. His mother also heard him screaming at night, saying, "Don't Matthew, stop!" Max also started having nightmares about blood, people dying, and vampires chasing him. His mother took him to the doctor and it was discovered that Max had tears in his anus. After his mother began to question him, Max disclosed that a 9-year-old boy, Matthew, had molested him twice on the bus and twice in the bathroom at school by penetrating his anus with his fingers. Clearly, the sexual abuse had a significant emotional impact on Max.

What Can You Do?

This is a tough question, as children need to attend school and it is often not possible to control your child's school environment. The key here is to educate your child about sexual abuse and encourage your child to tell you if they are ever sexually abused so you can intervene as soon as possible. You may not be able to control whether or not your child gets sexually abused, but you can take steps to make it more likely that your child will tell you as soon as it happens. This allows you to intervene quickly and take steps to prevent the abuse from occurring again. By doing so, you can minimize the potential emotional damage to your child. Having said that, we do recommend that you try to select the safest school environment possible for your child. This means selecting a school where the children are well-supervised, the staff are competent and attentive, and the children are generally well-behaved. We realize that many parents do not have the option to select their child's school, as the child may be required to attend the public school in their district, and the parent may not be able to move to a more desirable school district. In that case, the parents' primary focus should be on educating the child about abuse, making sure the child feels comfortable enough to report any abuse, and regularly checking in with the child about their experience at school. In all cases, the parents should be alert to any changes in the child's behavior, such as recent onset of bedwetting, aggressive behavior, sexual acting out, and so forth, as these are "red flags" of possible abuse or other stressors.

On the School Bus

This is another place where children of different ages often mix. While there is an adult driving the bus, there is often no other adult monitoring the children. We have seen numerous cases where children have exposed their genitals to other children on the bus, made sexual comments, and engaged in sexual activity with other children. Consider the case of Tina:

A 10-year-old boy fondled 5-year-old Tina on her vagina, and had Tina fondle him while they rode the school bus. Tina then later began fondling other girls in her neighborhood until one of those girls told.

What Can You Do?

The most obvious answer is to not have your children ride the school bus. If this is not possible, then encourage your child to sit at the front of the bus, as abuse is less likely to occur within possible eyesight of the bus driver. You can also encourage your child to sit next to children his age rather than with a much older child. Again, you should maintain an open line of communication with your child, and ask regularly about their school day, including their experiences on the bus, so you can catch any problems as they arise.

In the Classroom

It's hard to believe, but some children have actually been molested in the classroom when the teacher was present. As noted in Chapter 1, we saw a case where a 12-year-old boy molested a 7-year-old girl during his extracurricular club at a prestigious private school. He was able to put his finger into her vagina while she sat on his lap during the club. Although there were teachers in the room at the time, they could not see what was occurring under the table, and the girl did not tell because the boy had "groomed" her so well. This case highlights why we believe it is best to not group older children with much younger children. However, we have also had cases where children have molested other children of the same age in the classroom. The abuse often occurred during movies in class when the lights were off, or when teachers walked out of the room or turned their backs. Sexual abuse can also occur in classrooms even of very young children. Consider the case of Darryl in Pre-K:

During their Pre-K class, 5-year-old Darryl performed oral sex on 4-year-old Jarvis and made Jarvis perform oral sex on him.

This took place on multiple occasions in the boys' classroom during less structured portions of the day, including when they were in time-out together. Darryl told Jarvis, "if you let me do it to you, I'll let you do it to me." This is one way that sexually aggressive children try to coax other children into sexual contact. It is also a way to get the younger child to later feel guilty, as if they somehow agreed to the sexual touching. In this case, the touching was not consensual, and Darryl bullied Jarvis throughout the year. On one occasion, Darryl urinated on Jarvis's head when they were in the school bathroom. Around the time that the sexual abuse was occurring, Jarvis repeatedly complained of headaches and of not feeling well. He also wet his bed, bullied his younger brother, and showed cruelty to animals. On one occasion, Jarvis stuffed clothing into the front of his pants and stated, "I don't want anybody to touch my pee pee ever again." Jarvis never told about the sexual abuse, but his teachers finally discovered it.

As in the case of Jarvis above, it is quite common for children to not tell about sexual abuse, but to show many red flags that something is wrong. It is often up to the adults around the child to figure out what is going on.

What Can You Do?

As we said before, be sure to educate your child about sexual abuse and reassure your child that he or she will not get in trouble if they tell you about any abuse. Also, check in regularly with your child to see how they feel about school and the other children in their classroom. In addition, you should follow-up on any "red flags" or changes in your child's behavior that could be a sign that something is wrong. If your child's problems persist, then you should take your child to a counselor who specializes in treating children, and preferably, who has experience and training regarding sexual abuse.

In the Neighborhood

Sexual abuse can occur when younger children are playing with older children in the neighborhood, with little or no adult supervision. For example, a group of children in the neighborhood may gather together to play games in someone's backyard. Truth or Dare is a popular game that can often involve some sexual activity. While such play may be normal among children of similar age, it is not normal or healthy when older children initiate sexual activity with much younger children, as in the case below:

Jason is a 12-year-old boy who seemed particularly good with young children. The adults in the neighborhood liked him because he was always willing to babysit and play with the younger children. The younger children also looked up to him and wanted to spend time with him. Jason's father worked as a doctor and his mother was a legal secretary. Jason attended a private Christian school. Jason often played with 4-year-old Sam and 7-year-old Nick in his neighborhood. Sam and Nick's parents appreciated Jason's willingness to help out and play with their sons. One day, Sam and Nick's parents caught Sam and Nick touching each other on their penises. When asked where they learned to do that, they said that Jason had shown them. When questioned further, they revealed that Jason had performed oral and anal sex on both of them, and had them do these things to each other. Jason's parents were shocked and confused. Jason initially denied the touching, but later admitted to it. He indicated that he had bribed the boys into the touching by telling them that, if they did what he wanted, he would play their games with them. He admitted that the boys did whatever he asked because they looked up to him. He said that he did these sexual things to the boys when they were playing outside in his tree house.

Jason's case is a good example of "grooming," or how the older child manipulates the younger child into sexual activity. In this case, the older child groomed the younger children by offering to play their games with them. This case also illustrates how sexual abuse often occurs in a private place, such as a tree house, where parents are not likely to go. Other common places in the neighborhood for sexual abuse include "forts," tents, sheds, "clubhouses," basements, attics, empty homes, and any other area that is shielded from view. We have also seen cases where children molested other children under the trampoline, in the woods, behind a shed, and in the crawlspace under the house. Essentially, sexual abuse can occur anywhere that is out of direct view of adults.

At age 7, Sean was exposed to pornographic videos and magazines. Shortly thereafter, he started engaging in sexual activity with his 5-year-old neighbor, Amy. He had Amy suck his penis and then he anally penetrated her. He did this about 10 times in his bedroom and on her couch when her mother was asleep and her father was outside. Amy did not tell anyone so the sexual abuse continued until Sean and his family moved to another neighborhood. Like many sexual abuse victims, Amy waited until she felt safe from her abuser before she disclosed the abuse.

At the Babysitter's

Teens who molest younger children often offer to babysit children so they can molest them. Unfortunately, it can be hard to tell which teens are likely to molest children, as these teens tend to look "normal." Although the abusers are more likely to be boys, there are also girls who molest children, as in the case of Marissa:

15-year-old Marissa often babysat children in her neighborhood. While babysitting, she would show the children pornographic movies and then she would perform on the children the sexual acts depicted in the movies.

Many sexual abusers, regardless of their age, use pornography to get younger children to do sexual things. The younger children may think that it is okay to do the sexual things because they see the adults on the screen engaging in these behaviors.

Sexual abuse can occur not only by a child's babysitter, but also by an older child at the babysitter's house. Parents know to check out their child's babysitter, but most don't think to ask about any other children that might be present at the babysitter's house. We have seen many cases where a child was sexually abused or exposed to sexual material by an older child in their babysitter's home, such as the babysitter's own child, family member, friend or neighbor.

What Can You Do?

Be very careful when selecting a babysitter for your child. We recommend that you choose someone who you know well or who has been recommended to you by a trusted source. We also recommend that you avoid hiring teenage boys as babysitters. While most teenage boys are not likely to molest a younger child, there is a significant percentage who will, and those tend to be the teenage boys who volunteer to babysit. Keep in mind that most teenage boys have little to no interest in babysitting, and most would not actually volunteer to babysit, particularly if they are not being paid. Instead, most teens prefer to hang out with other teens, not with much younger children. So, if a teenage boy volunteers to babysit, then you should ask yourself why this might be the case. There may be legitimate reasons, but it may also be that the teenager has his own agenda. The agenda may not necessarily be to molest a child, but it may be to gain access to an internet-active computer with no parental controls that can allow him to view pornography. In this case, your child could end up being exposed to pornography. It is helpful to keep in mind the old adage, "if something seems too good to be true, it probably is." This is especially the case with child care. If someone is volunteering to take care of your children for free and for nothing in return, then you should be wary.

> *Ms. Smith allowed a male acquaintance of hers, Jack, to move into her home, as he volunteered to babysit her children. Ms. Smith was pleased that Jack seemed so interested in her children and he played with them constantly, in the pool, on the X-Box, and in the yard. This was a huge relief for Ms. Smith, as it was summer and she was tired of having to constantly entertain her children, particularly since she suffered from chronic joint pain and fatigue. When Ms. Smith's 4-year-old daughter, Suzy, told her that Jack had touched her "too too" when tucking her in bed, Ms. Smith simply could not believe it. She was sure that Jack was a nice man who would never do anything like that, and the children loved to play with him. It wasn't until 6 months later, when Suzy told her Pre-K teacher about the abuse that Ms. Smith began to consider that Suzy had told the truth.*

In addition to carefully screening your babysitter, you need to find out who is likely to be at the babysitter's house when your child is there, and what type of supervision will be provided. In particular, you need to know if there will be much older children, other adults, or children who have sexual behavior problems. Ideally, it is best to not have your child mixing with other children you do not know or whose parents you do not know, unless it is a carefully supervised setting where there is close adult supervision.

At a Friend's Home

We have seen many cases where sexual abuse occurred when the child was visiting their friends' homes, particularly when spending the night. Sometimes it was the friend who was the abuser whereas other times it was the friend's older sibling or parent. We have also seen cases where the abuse occurred in the child's own home.

10-year-old Sam had his 12-year-old friend, Evan, spend the night. Evan brought a pornographic video with him and they watched it in the living room once everyone else had gone to sleep. The video showed a brother and sister in their late teens engaging in fondling, anal sex, and oral sex with each other. Sam later molested his younger sister, repeating the sexual behaviors that he saw on the video.

What Can You Do?

You need to be careful about whose homes you allow your child to visit. We recommend that you not allow your child to go to someone's house unless you know the child and parent well, and you feel comfortable about the level of supervision provided there. We also recommend that you find out if your child will have access to the Internet or television without parental controls. As for children spending the night at your house, we recommend that you check on the children periodically and ensure there are parental controls on all of the televisions and internet-accessible devices in the home. You should also check to see if the child coming over has brought any internet-accessible devices such as cell phone or PSP. We also recommend that your child not spend the night with any child who is 3 or more years older, as there is likely to be a significant developmental and power difference between the two children (see Chapter 2 for more discussion about the significance of age differences between children).

On Playgrounds

Playgrounds can potentially be high-risk environments if older children are mixing with much younger children in areas that are shielded from view. For example, we have seen several cases where children were sexually abused by other children in the opaque play tubes at the playgrounds of fast-food restaurants.

What Can You Do?

We recommend that you not allow your child to go to the playground without you or another responsible adult. Once at the playground, you should keep an eye on your child and monitor who your child is playing with. In general, it is best if your child plays with children who are their age or near their age. If you notice that a much older child is interacting with your child, then watch the interaction closely. It might be helpful to go over to your child and check in. This will let the older child know that you are nearby and will reduce the risk of the older child trying to do anything inappropriate with your child.

When at a playground with opaque play tubes, we recommend that before allowing your children into the tubes that you check to see which other children are in the tubes. In general, it is best if your child is not in the tubes with much older children. We also recommend that you visually check on your child if your child and another child suddenly become quiet in the tubes and are staying in one location. Generally speaking, there is probably no need for concern if you can hear the children talking and moving about within the tubes, and their conversation is appropriate.

At Church

Many people, parents included, naturally consider their church to be a safe place. In our clinical experience, however, we have seen a number of cases where an older child sexually abused a younger child in a church setting. Earlier, we discussed the issue of church-run daycares. But there have been problems in other church situations as well, as in the case of Lindsay:

13-year-old Shaun often played with 4-year-old Lindsay at their church. Their parents were friends, and the families would spend most of their Sundays at church, during which time the children of all ages were allowed to socialize freely at the church, with little supervision. One day Lindsay put her hand down her pants during speech therapy and she was rubbing her vaginal area. When asked why she did this, Lindsay said that Shaun had been touching her privates at church. Lindsay's mother was shocked by this, as she said that everyone at their small church trusted each other, and she assumed that she could trust as well.

This case illustrates how children can be molested even in places that are considered to be safe and by people who are considered to be trustworthy. The sexual abuse in this case could have probably been prevented if the girl's parents had followed the general rule of not allowing their young child to be left unsupervised with a much older child, particularly a teenage boy.

What Can You Do?

You should treat church just as you would treat any other environment discussed in this chapter. In other words, don't assume that church is somehow exempt from the rules that apply in every other setting. There are abusers at church just as there are abusers everywhere else, and going to church doesn't reduce someone's risk of being an abuser. Just think about the highly publicized cases of sexual abuse perpetrated by Catholic priests. So, you should be careful at church about who you allow your child to be with, and make sure that there is sufficient adult supervision whenever young children are mixing with much older children.

At Home

We have listed a number of places outside of the home where sexual abuse can occur. But the truth is that sexual abuse often occurs right at home. This means that parents should not assume that their children are safe from sexual abuse at home. Children can be sexually abused at home by older siblings, other relatives, and people who live in the home or come to visit. So the same recommendations above apply to your own home.

What Can You Do?

Discourage the children in your home from playing behind closed doors, particularly if there is a large age difference between them. Check on your children regularly so you are aware of what they are doing. If they do start engaging in some inappropriate behavior, the sooner you intervene, the better.

Rule of Thumb to Avoid High Risk Situations

Avoid any place where your child:

- ✓ Receives little supervision around children who are 3 or more years older

- ✓ Receives little supervision around children who have been sexually abused and/or exposed to pornography or adult sexual activity

- ✓ Has access to porn on the Internet, TV, cell phone, PSP, or other electronic device

---

Part 2: The Child

For all the work a parent may do to make sure their child's environment is safe, there is simply no way they can ensure that their child will *never* be in a situation where they might be sexually abused. The last line of defense, in these cases, will be the child himself. Many parents are uncomfortable with the idea of talking about sexual abuse with their children. But it is important to remember that you can give your children essential information that will help them deal with situations where someone is trying to take advantage of them.

Ways to Arm Your Child Against Sexual Abuse

1) **Teach your children that their body belongs to them, and that they have a right to not be touched.**

    In order to teach this, we need to respect when our children say that they don't want to be touched, such as hugged or kissed. For example, we should not force or pressure our children to give a goodnight kiss to a relative if they don't want to. We should also not allow others to tickle, kiss, hug, pinch, or pick up our children if our children don't want this. By respecting our children's feelings about their bodies, we are teaching them that they have a right to refuse unwanted touch. This can help our children be more assertive in refusing any unwanted touch.

    You can also help your child understand this concept by reading them an educational book about boundaries, such as *No More Secrets For Me*. This book has stories that teach the concepts of privacy and personal boundaries. This book recommends that you tell your child, "Your body belongs to you. If anyone touches you in a way you don't like, it's OK to tell them you don't like it. And tell me too and I will tell them to stop it." [3]

2) **Educate your child about sexual abuse.**

    Explain to your child that there are private places on their body that others are not supposed to touch, except in certain circumstances, such as when they go to the doctor. Explain that it is wrong for adults and older children to sexually touch them, and such touching is against the rules or against the law. Make sure to teach your child specific words for their private parts so that your child is able to communicate clearly with you about any unwanted sexual touching they may receive. Many experts believe that parents should teach their children the anatomically correct names such as penis and vagina. However, we do not believe this is necessary in order for your child to later communicate about sexual abuse.

Tell your child he or she needs to let you know if someone touches their private parts, even if that person is a family member or friend. You can discuss these issues with your child by reading a book to them about touching such as *Your Body Belongs to You*. You can also buy a DVD containing the Good Touch/Bad Touch curriculum that is designed to help parents talk to their children about sexual abuse. This can be found at www.childhelpusa.org. For children under age 10, we recommend that you check in with your child periodically, about once a year, to make sure they still remember and understand what constitutes inappropriate touching. It is best if you can use everyday opportunities to discuss this subject with your children. Here is any example from my own personal experience with my 7-year-old daughter:

I recently took my daughters to play at a local park. While at the park, another parent told me that a man had been arrested for soliciting a child at this very park just two weeks before. Shortly after this, my 7-year-old daughter ran off with her friends, out of my sight. I followed my daughter, pulled her to the side, and reminded her that she needs to stay where I can see her. I reminded her that there are some adults and older children who do wrong things to children. I then told her about the man who had been arrested at that very park just 2 weeks before. My daughter then revealed that her friend had been at the park that day and had told her about seeing the man being taken off by the police. I talked with my daughter about how this man approached the little girl by saying "What a pretty dress you're wearing. Do you have pretty panties to match?" I explained how this may have been a way for him to get the girl to show her panties to him. I also explained that this man tried to get the girl to go off with him. My daughter then asked a lot of questions and we talked about various ways adults might try to trick a child into going off with them, such as asking for help to look for a missing puppy or asking the child to come to his car to get some candy. We then talked about what she could do in that situation, such as telling the man she is not supposed to talk to strangers and then walking away and telling a trusted adult immediately. My daughter practiced some of her responses and expressed confidence about her ability to set limits in such a situation.

3) **Teach your child about different types of feelings.**

Help your child learn to identify their feelings and talk about their feelings, such as feeling mad, sad, happy, or scared. There are various books and games you can use to educate your child about feelings. *Feelings* is a good book for teaching young children about feelings. This book has photos of children displaying different feelings. You can find other resources at www.do2learn.com. Also encourage your child to talk about how they feel when receiving different types of touches, such as how they feel when they are pushed, hit, or tickled against their will. This teaches children to trust their perceptions and feel comfortable verbalizing them.

4) Explain to your child that they should not keep secrets about touching.

Also explain to your child that if someone asks them to keep a secret about touching, then it is probably not good touching.

5) Tell your child to never get in a car with anyone without your permission, and to never walk off with anyone without your permission.

6) Make sure your child's emotional needs are getting met.

Children who are not getting their needs met by their family are more vulnerable to potential molesters, who may prey on the children by offering to meet those needs. Perpetrators with many victims are particularly skilled at picking out children who are both easier to manipulate and less likely to tell. These children tend to be quiet and shy, with few friends and with relatively poor relationships with their parents. The perpetrator may offer to be the child's "special friend," giving the child a sense of belonging and worth that he will later exploit to molest the child.

Are My Child's Emotional Needs Being Met?

Does my child:

☐ Have friends?
☐ Feel like I love him?
☐ Feel good about himself?
☐ Engage in activities that make him feel happy?
☐ Get to spend individual quality time with me or his other parent each day?

Children whose emotional needs are not getting met are more vulnerable to abusers, as well as more likely to develop emotional and behavioral problems.

Parenting Styles

One of the most important ways you can help your child get his emotional needs met is to have a good relationship with your child. In general, parents who adopt a particular parenting style are more likely to have good relationships with their children. The idea of parenting styles was first developed by psychologist Diana Baumrind in the 1960s.[4] Dr. Baumrind determined that there were 3 distinct styles of parenting – Authoritative, Authoritarian, and Permissive. These different styles are distinguished from each other by two major factors – how much control the parent exercises over their child, and how much warmth and genuine communication is expressed between the parent and child. As the theory has developed, a fourth style of parenting – Neglectful – was added.[5] These different styles matter, because of the effect they have on the children who are raised under them. Here is a summary of each style:

Authoritarian

"You're going to Harvard, and you're going to be a doctor." – Mr. Perry to his aspiring actor son, *Dead Poets Society* (1989)

The authoritarian parent subscribes to a sort of "police officer" view of parenting. This parent exercises a high degree of control over their child. However, there is a corresponding lack of warmth and communication in the parent-child relationship. Authoritarian parents do not explain why they are restricting their child from a particular activity. Instead, they just tell the child "because I said so." These parents may take it as a sign of weakness to have to explain their reasoning to their child. They also have very high expectations for their child's behavior, demanding that even young children act like "little adults." Many children raised with this style view their parents' edicts as being unfair and arbitrary. They do not see any wisdom in the restrictions imposed on them, and they may act out as a form of rebellion. These children may view the parent as an unreachable, unreasonable force in their life, and may not go to the parent with any problems or worries because of the conviction that the parent "just doesn't get it." Other times, children raised in such homes will have low self-esteem and a lack of independence, because they have become used to their parents making all their choices for them – including what their career is going to be and whom they can marry.

Permissive

"An infallible way to make your child miserable is to satisfy all his demands."
Henry Home, Scottish jurist and philosopher (1696 - 1782)

The permissive parent (also sometimes referred to as "indulgent") expresses considerable warmth towards their child, but exercises very little control. Children raised in authoritarian households may grow up to be permissive parents, because they are determined to not be like their parents. Permissive parents want a close relationship with their child, and sometimes have difficulty exercising control because of a fear that their child will not like them if they do so. Permissive parents want to be "buddies" with their children, instead of actual parents. The lack of control they exercise can lead their children to be impulsive and spoiled, simply because these children have learned that they get whatever they want, and quickly. Children from permissive homes are also more likely to avoid taking responsibility for their actions, having become used to their parents making excuses for them. As these children grow up, they are more likely to be immature, have low academic and work achievement, and have substance abuse problems.

Neglectful

"I hate fathers, and I never wanted to be one." - Steve Zissou, *Life Aquatic with Steven Zissou* (2004)

Neglectful parents do not exercise control over their children, and do not express much if any warmth or affection towards them. Oftentimes neglectful parents did not really want to be parents in the first place, and see their children as unwelcome impediments in their lives. It should be noted that in this situation "neglectful" does not necessarily mean neglecting the basic needs of the child, such as food or clothing. Rather, it means neglecting the emotional needs of the child as well as their need for structure and guidance. Neglectful parents are much more focused on their own needs, rather than the needs of their children. The children themselves are keenly aware of this disparity, and often perceive themselves as being an unwanted burden to their parents. Children who grow up in neglectful homes may have significant emotional and behavioral problems, because they lack the emotional bonding so critical in early childhood development.

Authoritative

"Live so that when your children think of fairness and integrity, they think of you." –   H. Jackson Brown

The authoritative parent exercises a significant degree of control over their child, but they also express considerable warmth and affection towards them. Authoritative parents set clear expectations and limits for their children. They try to explain to their child why they are restricting them from a particular activity, or why they need them to behave in a certain way. The children receive consequences for misdeeds, but also constant reassurance as to their self-worth and the parent's love for them. Children from authoritative homes are more likely to internalize their parents' sense of structure and carry it into their own lives once they achieve independence. The authoritative style is sometimes referred to as the "democratic" style, because as children get older their parents negotiate with them to increase their freedom and responsibilities. There will still be a fair amount of conflict between the parent and child in an authoritative home – such is the nature of parent/child relationships. But research has consistently shown that children from authoritative homes tend to be more successful and have fewer significant problems than children from authoritarian, permissive, or neglectful homes.

Conclusion

While there is no way to guarantee that your child will never be sexually abused, parents can dramatically reduce the risk to their children by taking an active interest in both the people and places their child will be interacting with. Parents can also reduce the risk to their children by communicating clearly with them about sexual abuse. Finally, those parents who have an authoritative parenting style are more likely to have strong relationships with their children, which can also help reduce the child's risk of being sexually abused.

Books to Help Parents Talk to Their Children About Inappropriate Touching

Federico, Julie. (2008). Some Parts are Not for Sharing. Tate Publishing.

Freeman, Lory. (1984) It's MY Body: A Book to Teach Young Children How to Resist Uncomfortable Touch (Parents Guide). Parenting Press: Seattle, WA.

Girard, Linda. (1984). My Body is Private. Albert Whitman & Company.

Hindman, Jan. (1983) A Very Touching Book...for Little People and Big People. Alexandria Assoc..

Spelman, Cornelia. (1997). Your Body Belongs to You. Albert Whitman & Company.

Stauffer, L. & Deblinger, E. (2003). Let's Talk About Taking Care of You: An Educational Book About Body Safety. Hatfield, PA: Hope for Families.

Stauffer, Lori & Deblinger, E. (2004) Let's Talk About Taking Care of You: An Educational Book about Body Safety for Young Children. Hope for Families, Inc.: Hatfield, PA. [toddlers version]

Stauffer, Lori & Deblinger, E. (2004) Let's Talk About Safety Skill for Kids: A Personal Safety Activity Book for Parents and Children. Hope for Families, Inc.: Hatfield, PA. [elementary version]

Wachter, Oralee. (2002). No More Secrets for Me. Little, Brown and Company.

[1] Darkness to Light (2007). *Stewards of Children: Adults Protecting Children from Sexual Abuse.*

[2] Abel, G.G. & Harlow, N. *The Stop Child Molestation Book* (2001)

[3] Watcher, O. (2002). *No More Secrets for Me,* Little, Brown.

[4] Baumrind, D. (1966). Effects of Authoritative Parental Control on Child Behavior, *Child Development, 37(4),* 887-907.

[5] Maccoby, EE and Martin, JA. (1983). Socialization in the context of the family: Parent–child interaction. In P Mussen and EM Hetherington, editors, *Handbook of Child Psychology, Volume IV: Socialization, Personality, and Social Development,* chapter 1, pages 1–101. New York: Wiley, 4th edition

Chapter 7: Keeping Your Kids Away From Pornography

Introduction – Selling Sex

People have been producing stories and images about sex for probably about as long as sex has been around. It wasn't until the 1960s, however, that selling sex in the form of pornography became a genuine industry in the United States. The advent of magazines such as *Playboy* and *Penthouse* brought pornographic photos into the mainstream. The advent of the VCR brought pornographic movies into people's homes. And the advent of the Internet made pornography widely and easily available to anyone with a computer. Philosophy majors may want to argue over the artistic merits of porn, or how it is a sign of a new "sexual freedom." However, the bottom line behind its manufacture has been, and always will be, about money. Selling sex is big business in America, and the main reason behind the incredible proliferation of pornography over the past 10 to 20 years is that it is very, very popular. Not surprisingly, pornography has become increasingly popular with children as well.

Parents today who can remember sneaking a peek at their dad's Playboys may think that their children seeing porn is not really a big deal. They may even see it as a rite of passage. The experience we have in working with children and adolescents today, however, teaches us that children are being exposed to hard-core pornography earlier, and at a greater intensity and frequency, than ever before.

Such exposure can lead children to act out sexually, and to engage in sexual behaviors that even their parents may have never experienced. There are sites devoted exclusively to incest, rape, bondage, sadomasochism, bestiality, and child molestation. There are adolescents who have become addicted to Internet pornography, viewing it to the exclusion of social activities, family, and school. Adolescents may also have their sexuality shaped by the images and videos they have seen, believing them to be accurate depictions of what a sexual relationship is really like. The truth is, pornography can have a devastating effect on the sexual development of children and adolescents. As technology has made it easier for people to access pornography, parents have a vested interest in blocking that access wherever it is possible.

Keeping Your Home "Clean"

Magazines and Videos:

As an adult, the easiest step to keeping pornography from your children is to not have any of your own. We have seen many, many cases of children getting access to pornography that belonged to their parents. In some cases the parents simply had the pornography laying out for anyone to see. In other cases, the parents thought they had their pornography well hidden, but their child had discovered the hiding place and was regularly looking at the pornography without their knowledge. If you do have pornography in your home, you should keep it in a locked cabinet – and keep the key with you at all times.

At age 10, Jack found pornographic magazines in his parents' room, under their bed. He later found a pornographic video in his father's drawer when looking for socks, and went back to his parents' room to look for more pornographic videos and ended up watching these movies hundreds of times. Jack later molested his younger sister. He said that he wanted to do the sexual things he had seen in the magazines and movies.

Keep in mind that even if you do not have any pornography in your house, your child may find it elsewhere. There have been cases of children coming across pornographic pictures or magazines lying on the ground, in abandoned houses, in the woods, in garbage cans, and so on. Children often get pornography from their friends, or acquaintances from school. One child we saw talked about an older boy at school who was selling pornographic DVDs that he got from his adult brother. Other children at school have sold pornographic pictures torn out from magazines or printed off the Internet.

Television:

There are many ways that children can view pornography, or highly sexualized material, on television. Satellite and cable television companies almost always offer pornographic channels as part of their programming, and pay-per-view services provide another opportunity to view pornographic movies. We strongly recommend that parents not put digital, satellite, or cable TV in their children's bedrooms since this can provide easy access to sexually explicit programming. We have seen many cases where parents had no idea that their children could access pornographic movies on the movie channels late at night.

The parents also thought that their children were asleep when such movies were showing, only to later discover that the children were getting up in the middle of the night and turning off the volume so the parents wouldn't know they were watching TV. We have also seen cases where the children would watch blocked pornographic channels that were fuzzy, but showed some flashes of picture as well as sound. Although the visual quality was poor, the children still saw and heard sexual material.

In addition to the hard-core programming that is potentially available on television, mainstream cable channels may offer shows that are profoundly inappropriate for children. Parents are recommended to monitor their child's viewing – even of children's channels – as they may contain inappropriate shows. Take the Cartoon Network, for example. Late at night, there are sexually violent cartoons on this channel during the Adult Swim programming. These cartoons depict rape and sexual violence and are completely inappropriate for children.

We have had several adult sex offenders in our treatment program who have failed their polygraphs because they were watching these pornographic cartoons. They failed the polygraph because one of the questions they are asked is if they were complying with the conditions of treatment and probation, which prohibit them from viewing pornography. We have also had several cases of children who were acting out sexually who reported having learned about sex from watching Adult Swim at night in their bedrooms, without their parents' knowledge. Thus, it is really not safe to put cable TV in your child's bedroom and assume that they cannot access sexually explicit programming on basic cable stations.

Other People's Homes:

Many of the parents we work with express frustration over the subject of other people's homes. The following example does a pretty good job illustrating why:

"Harry" is a 13-year-old boy in treatment for sexually harassing girls at his school. His mother, Mrs. "Smith," indicated that she worked hard to restrict access to inappropriate material in her home. Harry confirmed that his parents took extensive measures to prevent him from accessing pornography at their house. So he would go to his aunt's house instead. Her computer had no blocking software, and her teenaged son had an impressive collection of

pornographic DVDs that he loaned to Harry on a regular basis.

A parent can feel helpless when they do all the right things, only to have their children exposed to all the wrong things by simply going across the street. They may also get angry with the parents of the other home, thinking them neglectful at best and malicious at worst. In our experience, most of the time when a child is exposed to pornography at someone else's home, it is due to the adults in that home simply not being aware of the risks involved. In some cases the adult in question has no children of their own, and so they have not even considered the issue of children accessing pornography. There have been cases, however, where the child was intentionally exposed to pornography by adults in another home.

> *"Sam" is an 11-year-old boy who has problems acting out sexually. Over the course of treatment, Sam talked about how he would spend much time over the summer at his grandmother's house. Also living in that house was Sam's 20-year-old cousin "Jake." Jake would often be put in charge of looking after Sam. Jake looked at pornographic movies frequently, and invited Sam to watch the movies with him. According to Sam, Jake never molested him or exposed himself. Nonetheless, Jake's intentionally exposing Sam to pornography proved to be a major factor in Sam's sexual acting out.*

In today's world, parents cannot take it for granted that their child will be safe in someone else's home. We recommend that you not allow your children to go to other people's houses without you unless you know those people very well, and you feel confident that your child will not be exposed to any inappropriate sexual material or activity in that home. Before allowing your child to go over to someone's house by themselves, you should be able to answer the following about the parents in that home:

- Do they have parental blocks on their internet-active computers?
- Do they have any pornography locked up so that the children cannot find it?
- Are there any older children in the home who have a history of molesting younger children?
- Do they allow their children and their children's friends to watch R-rated movies that contain sexual content?
- Do they allow their children and their children's friends to play with other children in the neighborhood without adult supervision?
- Do they lock their bedroom doors when undressing or engaging in sexual activity?

Parents may be somewhat daunted and embarrassed at the prospect of trying to find out this information about a particular home. Some may take the approach that they won't go looking for problems unless something comes up. Remember, though, that this is about your child's safety and well-being. It's worth a little embarrassment to gain some peace of mind. And if any adult or parent takes offense at your asking such questions, make sure to let them know that *they* are entitled to ask those exact same questions about *your* home.

It's also a good idea to expose your child to a positive peer group as much as possible and minimize any contact with a negative peer group. Get to know your child's friends and their parents, and encourage your child's friendships with those who are positive influences. Look for parents who have similar values to you and who are also concerned about what their children are exposed to.

The Internet

There is no question that the Internet has revolutionized how information and entertainment are created and distributed. Children today consider the Internet a natural part of daily life, like television. Like learning a new language, those lucky enough to grow up after the advent of the Internet can navigate it with the same ease as channel surfing. Their parents, however, are very likely to be less fluent in its use. For those of us born in the 60s and 70s, learning how to use computers is much like trying to learn a second language after you're grown. This is particularly troublesome when it comes to protecting your children from the potential harm that the Internet can bring right into your home. Many of the parents we have worked with admit they have no idea what their children are doing online, and they often have no idea how easy it is for their children to access so-called "adult" content.

Imagine that a new business opens right next door to your home. You soon discover that the business sells pornographic images and videos. It has a wide range of products, encompassing just about every sexual variation you can imagine (and quite a few you can't). There is even a section of the store that sells child pornography, for those willing to invest a little more effort. The store will sell to anyone that can pay, regardless of age. It has a huge amount of free samples that it willingly distributes, and puts elaborate flyers advertising its products in your mailbox on a regular basis. Most parents facing such a situation would be understandably alarmed by the presence of such a store in their neighborhood. They might petition the city to revoke the store's business license, on the grounds that its presence puts their children at unnecessary risk for exposure to inappropriate material.

The sad truth is, such a store already exists – not as a physical "brick and mortar" store, but as the huge variety of web sites that traffic and trade in pornography. Pornography is a huge business in this country – worth 13 *billion* dollars a year according to a 2006 review.[1] According to that same review, over 28,000 Internet users *per second* are looking at Internet pornography.[2] It is estimated that Internet pornography raises 2.5 billion dollars of revenue yearly.[3]

From a business point of view, it makes sense that the easier it is for potential consumers to gain access to your product, the more money you will make. Thus, the pornography industry has a vested interest in making it as easy as possible for people to view their product – including giving out free samples. This has naturally made it easier for children to access pornography as well. While some pornographic sites make an effort to restrict their content, the vast majority of these sites have no meaningful way to keep minors from viewing them. Many sites have nothing more than a screen advising the user that they must be at least 18, and if they are not, they need to leave. Even the most secure sites will let you have full access if you have a valid credit card – and there is no effort to verify that the person entering the card's information is the actual owner of the card.

All Internet sites have a "domain" as part of their address. Most Internet sites have ".com" at the end, which stands for "company." Government sites are followed by ".gov," professional organizations by ".org," schools by ".edu," and so on. At the time of this writing, a ".xxx" domain was recently approved for use by adult Internet sites (although there are still apparently some additional bureaucratic steps to take before the domain becomes active). The intention, apparently, is to provide pornography sites with a domain of their own.

In theory, this would help parents a great deal. It would make it much easier for parents to block access to pornographic sites. Unfortunately, it is unlikely that the ".xxx" domain is going to change things very much. Pornographic sites are not required to use the domain; it is merely an option. Attempts to force pornographic sites to use the .xxx domain would undoubtedly result in lawsuits and legal challenges. Some adult websites have already balked at the idea of using the .xxx domain, for the obvious reason that it would make blocking their sites both easier and more likely.[4] The bottom line is that parents cannot rely on the .xxx domain to help them identify inappropriate websites.

How Do Kids Access Porn on the Internet?

Internet Browsers:

The most common means of gaining access to pornography on the Internet is by the use of an Internet browser. The major browsing program for Windows-based computers is Internet Explorer, while the major program for Mac computers is called Safari. There are three ways of navigating to any particular website on the Internet. One way is to type the "address" of the site in the browser's address window (usually located at the top of the browser window). A second way is to use a search engine (such as Yahoo! and Google) to look for a particular site or sites that have certain content. A third way is to click on a "link" on your current web page, which then takes you to the site that the link goes to. Most browsers keep track of the sites you have gone to by compiling a list, which is usually referred to as the "history."

The adolescents we have worked with who use a browser to access porn usually begin by searching for sites that deal with sex, or whatever variation of sex they are interested in. For example, a particular adolescent may start on the "Google" search page and type in "sex videos." Google will then produce a list of sites that have such content (a recent search we made of that very term in Google produced a list of *12,100,000* different websites – the first offered "Full Free Porn Videos and DVDs").

The adolescent will usually go to various sites on the list, looking for free content. Most of these sites have links to other porn sites, also offering free content. A child or adolescent can spend literally hours clicking on various links and going from site to site. They may print out some of the pictures they see, or they may copy certain photos and video clips to the computer's hard drive or a portable "thumb drive" so they can view this material later on, without needing to be online to do so.

Adolescents who can access pornography in their own home are more likely to spend extended periods of time doing so, because they typically have more extended access to the computer. If a child's Internet access is restricted at home, however, he or she often manages to find an unrestricted computer by simply going to a friend or relative's house.

In our experience, the second-most common location where adolescents access Internet porn is school. Most schools now have some form of computer lab, and many have Internet access. You would think that schools would be particularly cautious about their students accessing pornography on school computers, but we have seen many cases where students have accessed pornography – even child pornography – at school. In some cases it is as simple as waiting for the computer teacher to leave the room briefly. The student only needs enough time to navigate to a site and download photos to the computer's hard drive, which can then be transferred to a floppy disk or thumb drive. While schools are increasingly using filtering programs such as NetNanny, there are various ways to defeat such programs (which will be discussed later in this chapter).

Another location where children can access Internet pornography is the library. The American Library Association's official position opposes any kind of filtering or blocking software on library computers, on the grounds that blocking any "Constitutionally protected speech" available on the Internet violates the First Amendment – their website has a formal resolution stating this.[5] A news story from Dallas in January 2008 noted how the lack of filters affected the cities' libraries:

> An analysis by *The Dallas Morning News* suggests tens of thousands of pornographic images pop up on Internet workstations every day at Dallas' 26 branch libraries. On December 19, in just a 45-minute span, computer users at the Central branch visited about 69,000 Web sites, which included more than 5,000 sites that were judged to be pornographic in nature. The sites included full nudity and sexual acts.[6]

Wireless Access or "Wi Fi":

It used to be that if you wanted to connect to the Internet, you needed a modem and a phone line that was physically connected to your computer. Modern technology has now given us wireless Internet access. Wireless Internet access is basically like a two-way radio, sending and receiving information without the need for physical wires to carry the information. You may have heard of "wi fi hot spots." These are areas that offer a wireless connection to the Internet. For example, many coffee shops in the US offer wireless Internet access (it is often prominently advertised). Somewhere in the shop there is a computer with a device that can broadcast and receive wireless signals. If you are close enough to this device, and if you have the proper equipment, you can get on the Internet. Most modern laptop computers have wireless capability built-in.

Go to your average Starbucks and you'll see a fair number of people there with laptops, using the shop's wireless access to surf the Internet. Many airports and hotels also offer wireless Internet access. Sometimes the service is free; other times you have to pay a fee in order to use it. There are a number of services online that keep track of wireless access points for any given area; one website lists many different free access points just for the Atlanta, Georgia region.[7] More and more portable devices are including the ability to connect to the Internet using wireless access, including several portable game devices (see below).

It is becoming more and more common for private residences to also have wireless Internet access. Typically this happens when someone in the home buys what is known as a "router." The router is a device that allows multiple computers in the home to share the same Internet connection. Most routers now also offer wireless access. The problem is, anyone with a computer that can detect wireless signals could potentially use that router to access the Internet, whether the owner of the router wants them to or not. This problem can be solved by restricting access to the router by using a password.

Not everyone restricts their access, however, either because they don't know how or simply don't want to bother with it. A person could drive or walk around neighborhoods looking for unrestricted wireless access spots, which they could then use to get access to the Internet. In some cases, however, a person doesn't even have to leave his or her own home to access another home's router. Look at the following diagram:

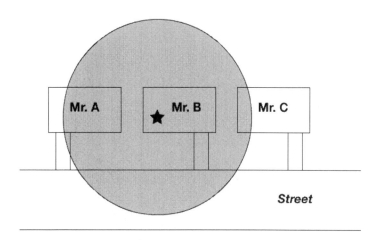

In this diagram, Mr. B has purchased an Internet router that includes wireless access. The router's location in Mr. B's house is marked with the star, and the circle around it is the range. Anyone within the circle, including those parts of the homes on either side, could use the router themselves to access the Internet, if they have a device that has "wi fi" capability.

Let's say that Mr. B has not taken the trouble to restrict access to his router by the use of a password. Mr. C has a child with a laptop computer, which when turned on automatically scans for available wi fi hot spots. The child could make use of Mr. B's router to view pornographic web sites, and to download pornography directly to his laptop – he could do this from the comfort of his own home. The problem of unrestricted wi fi access points is compounded in urban areas, where many individual residences coexist in a relatively small area. A typical apartment building could have as many overlapping wi fi access points as there are apartments.

File Sharing or "Peer-to-Peer" Networks:

More and more adolescents are gaining access to pornography through the use of so-called peer-to-peer networks. Most content online is accessed by connecting to a "server," which is basically a big computer dedicated to hosting a particular web site or sites. Peer-to-peer networks, however, involve connecting to other private computers online in order to "share" photos, videos, and music. Probably the most famous peer-to-peer network was Napster, which once allowed private users to download music without actually paying for it (Napster has since changed its format and no longer allows this). Typically, one begins using a peer-to-peer network by downloading a software program that facilitates connecting to the network. One major example is called "BitTorrent." Once the program is downloaded and installed, the user begins to search for files they are interested in – these files can be photographs, cartoon images, video clips, music files, or text files.

Once the user has found a file or files they want, they signal the program to begin downloading the file from other private computers on the network that have these files available for sharing. The program and files are all free – no credit cards or other form of payment is required. Needless to say, there is also no method for determining if the person downloading the file is a minor. The material available on such networks includes the full gamut of pornography. A child or adolescent may start using such services to download music, but it does not take long for them to realize that they can also download pornography. We have seen several cases where adolescents downloaded large amounts of child pornography using peer-to-peer networks. Sometimes the adolescent was not looking specifically for child pornography, but once they started viewing it they developed an interest and began seeking it out.

There is one aspect of peer-to-peer networks that all parents need to be aware of. Once you download the software and connect to the network, you are now part of the network. This means that any file you have downloaded is potentially available for other members of the network to download as well – from you. Thus, an adolescent who has downloaded child pornography from a peer-to-peer network, and who remains on the network, is now also distributing the child pornography to anyone who wants it. Adolescents have been charged with distribution of child pornography – a much more serious charge than possession – because they were using a peer-to-peer network to download it. Adolescents may have no idea others are using their computer to access child pornography, but such ignorance will not protect them in a court of law.

Game Systems:

The "Big 3" of home gaming systems as of this writing are the Xbox 360, PlayStation 3, and the Wii. The PS3 offers Internet access right out of the box. The Wii has a so-called "Internet channel," which is really a web browser. The Xbox 360 does not offer Internet access as a given, but there is a software program that can be downloaded for free from the Internet that puts a web browser on the system, which can then be used to view web sites.

Each one of these systems, then, could potentially be used to view pornographic web sites. The Xbox 360, PS3, and Wii each have wi fi capability. The Wii and PS3 have this capability out of the box, while the Xbox 360 needs an adapter that is plugged into the console's back. The fact that each of these consoles can access the Internet wirelessly is important, because a parent may believe that their child's console having Internet access is irrelevant because it is not connected to the Internet in their house.

However, if there is a neighbor who has an unrestricted router, the console could be used to access the Internet by using the neighbor's router. For example, refer back to the diagram above. Say that Mr. A's family has a Wii game system that is set up in their home, but within the range of Mr. B's router. Anyone in that home would be able to use the Wii to browse the Internet, including pornographic web sites. We have worked with parents who had no idea that their Wii had Internet capability. However, there is a way to restrict access to the Wii's browser (see below), just as there is with the PS3's browser. The PlayStation Portable, more commonly referred to as the PSP, also has a web browser installed. The device can access the Internet if it has a wireless connection available. Because of the portability of the device, it would be much easier for the user to make use of unrestricted wireless access points to get access to Internet pornography. Incredible as it may seem, there are websites dedicated to providing pornographic movies that have been formatted specifically for the PSP. Fortunately for parents, there is a way to disable the Internet browser on the device (see below).

The other major handheld gaming device is the Nintendo DS. The original DS also has wireless capability, but it cannot get on the Internet unless you have a special cartridge with the browser software on it. The browser was developed by the makers of the Opera web browser, and has an option to implement parental controls. The DS Internet cartridge was not a big hit and is no longer available for sale in the United States, but still can be purchased online. The updated version of the DS, called the DSi, also has wireless capability, and users can download a web browser for free from Nintendo's online store.

Cell Phones:

Cell phones have advanced by leaps and bounds since most adults first started using them. Many cell phones offer

Internet access, although the phones that do so usually cost more. However, as the technology improves it is becoming easier and cheaper to put small Internet browsers on phones. Many web providers have specially formatted "mobile" sites that accommodate cell phones' tiny screens. The porn industry, never one to ignore a potential means of selling to the public, has also provided web sites specifically designed for cell phones. We have seen more and more cases of children using cell phones to gain access to pornography. If their own phone does not have a web browser, they steal their parents' phones. Parents whose cell phones have web browsers would be well advised to keep the phone in their own room at night.

> *"John," a 15-year-old boy, was evaluated after he made terroristic threats at his school and was arrested. His mother also reported that he appeared to be preoccupied with sex. She reported that one day she noted that her cell phone's battery was dead, even though she had a full charge when she went to bed. When she charged the phone again, she saw that someone had used the phone to download pornographic pictures. It turned out that John was getting up at night and taking the phone –which the mother kept in the kitchen – to view pornographic sites. As it happened, John had been doing this for some time. His being caught was the result of 2 factors: he forgot to plug the phone back into the charger one night, and he had accidentally downloaded 2 pictures directly to the phone's memory. Had he not made these mistakes, his mother may have never discovered his behavior.*

Even if your child's phone does not offer Internet access, there is an excellent chance that it offers some form of instant messaging service. This service allows cell phone users to type short text messages and send them to people in their phone's address book. This process is preferred by teens to email because it is faster and easier to use. This is typically referred to as "texting."

The service that allows transmission of text is known as SMS, which stands for "Short Message Service." A relatively new service that is becoming more and more common is MMS, which is "Multimedia Message Service." This is a texting service that also allows the user to send pictures, music, and movie clips through the service.

With messaging services, you would think that the main concern is your child getting sent a pornographic image or text message from a friend – so-called "sexting," which is addressed in a later part of this chapter. However, there is a feature in SMS and MMS known as the *short code*. Normally, if you want to send someone a text message you first type in his or her telephone number so the phone knows where to send the message. Short codes are essentially abbreviated phone numbers (5 or 6 numbers long in the United States) belonging to various businesses, allowing a cell phone user to access content by texting to that code.

For example, a cell phone user might learn that a news organization is offering updates to the presidential election results. If the user wants to have those updates sent to their phone, they type in a short text message to the news organization's short code. "American Idol" makes extensive use of short codes for its voting procedure, where viewers can text to a certain singer's code to "vote" for them.

Texting to short codes usually costs more to the user than texting to private cell phone numbers, but not by a great amount. As you might have guessed by now, there are businesses selling pornography that have their own short codes. The code could be used to have pornographic content sent to the phone. The code could also be used in conjunction with a pornographic web site – for example, the cell phone user could text to the site's short code to get an access code, which they could then use to get into the pornographic site's premium content.

As more and more new cell phone users are finding out, when you buy a cell phone and get a new number, it isn't as "new" as you might think. As soon as a number is deactivated, it is put back in the hopper to be recycled for a new user. In February 2009, a 10-year-old boy got quite a shock when he was given a cell phone for his birthday. Among its many features, the phone offered MMS service, and the very day the boy got it he was sent a pornographic message – complete with pictures and audio, no less. It seems that the phone's previous owner had subscribed to a pornographic business that sent these messages. Parents giving their children a new cell phone may want to hang on to it for a few days first, to make sure no such "surprises" are forthcoming.

Signs that Someone Has Used Your Computer to Access Pornography

Pornographic Emails

Most everyone at some point has received unsolicited emails that contain pornographic content. However, if you start getting a number of such messages each time you check your email, there is a good chance that at some recent point someone has viewed a pornographic website using your computer.

Pornographic Pop-Up Ads

Pop-up ads are not as much a problem as they used to be, because current Internet browsers have built-in methods to block such ads. However, programs known as spyware or adware (see below) can throw up such ads even if they are normally blocked. Certainly if you normally block pop-ups, and you suddenly start getting pornographic pop up ads, that is a clear sign that someone has been tampering with your computer in some fashion.

Viruses and Spyware

The great majority of pornographic websites are not professional sites, but rather cheap sites that in all likelihood were thrown together very quickly. Porn sites have proven to be a haven for viruses, because people who go to such sites are usually pretty indiscriminate about what they click on and download. In addition, many of these sites will put little programs on your computer without your knowledge or consent. These programs come in 3 different varieties – spyware, adware, and malware.

Spyware – These programs are designed to collect information about what the user does while online. They keep logs of all the websites visited, and then transmit that information to a remote computer. Companies use this information to keep track of a person's viewing and buying habits. Some spyware programs can directly affect your Internet use – for example, you could type a search term into Google, and the spyware will reroute you to sites that they want you to go to.

Adware – These programs are designed to put advertising on your computer whether you want to see it or not. They are usually part of an application that the user downloads and installs in their computer. Some pornographic sites will get a user to download adware (and spyware, for that matter) by telling them they "need" the program to view certain video clips.

Malware – This is short for "malicious software," and is often used to refer to many different programs, including spyware. The most dangerous forms of malware, however, are those that allow outsiders to find out your passwords, and which can put viruses on your computer. Some programs are called "keyloggers," and they keep track of every keystroke you make. A savvy criminal can examine the log and determine what your likely passwords are.

Credit Card Bills

This one is kind of a no-brainer, but it does require careful checking of your credit card statements each month. Because a lot of pornographic sites want to encourage customers to sign up for premium content, they may indicate that the bill sent to the user's credit card account will have a non-sexual name – just in case the user in question has an inquisitive spouse, say. So a user will sign up to a porn site that is called "Lusty XXX Teens," but the bill has a name like "Cybervistas." The bottom line is, check your credit card bills for any charges that you don't recall making yourself.

"Red Flag" Terms

If you are checking your computer's browser history to see what your children have been looking at, you may want to look out for terms that relate to explicit sexual content. A lot of these terms are fairly obvious, for example "porn," "xxx," "erotica," and so on. But other terms won't mean much and might seem harmless unless you know what they are really about. Some of these terms are listed here.

Hentai – This term refers to a kind of Japanese animation or cartoon. You may have heard the term "Manga," which also refers to Japanese comics or animation. Some fairly well known Manga include Dragonball Z and Robotech (just a side note here: "Dragonball Z" is the mainstream animated program, and it is not sexual, but "Dragonball X" is a knock-off variation that is sexually explicit). Most Manga does not have hard-core sexual content. Hentai, on the other hand, is Japanese animation that is sexually explicit.

You may think that American pornography is explicit and disturbing, but it pales next to some of the material that the Japanese have come up with. There are animated films that show demons or alien beings raping women by using tentacles as if they were a penis. In fact, there is a whole subculture of Japanese porn that is called "naughty tentacles" or "tentacle rape." Hentai can be also be disturbing because the female models often look like children, even if the story says they are 18 or older.

Ecchi – This term refers to another kind of Japanese animation. While hentai usually refers to hard-core sexual material, ecchi typically refers to animation that has more "soft core" sexual content. While ecchi typically does not show sexual penetration, it is still highly sexualized.

Comixx or Comixxx – What a difference an extra "x" can make! "Comix" with one x is a commonly used word that refers to mainstream comic books or pictures. However, add one or two x's to the word, and it refers to comic images that are sexually explicit. So if you do a Google search for "comix," you will be directed to sites dealing with mainstream comic book images. Do a search for "comixx" on the other hand, and you will be directed to sites that have pornographic animation or comic books.

Among the material available are images showing popular Disney characters (such as Ariel, Belle, and Jasmine) in explicit sexual situations. It is important to note that more and more cartoon images depicting children in sexual situations have become available, and can be accessed more easily than child pornography involving photographs or video clips. This is because cartoon images of children are *not* considered child pornography under the law. However, from a treatment standpoint we consider cartoon images of children in sexual situations to be just as dangerous, because they still foster the perception of children as being capable and willing of engaging in sexual behavior with adults or older children. Such images also encourage the viewer to think of children as engaging in the full range of sexual behaviors, including intercourse and oral sex.

Controlling Your Child's Internet Access

Administrator Privileges

When a person buys a computer, takes it home, and sets it up for the first time, the computer's operating software (usually some form of "Windows") will have the person set up what is called a "user account." The first account that is created will have "Administrator" privileges.

Having Administrator privileges means that the user can select all the options for their computer, including for example whether or not to allow pop-up advertising in their Internet browser. The user will also be able to install new software on the computer, or uninstall software they do not want or need. If the person does not set up any additional user accounts, then anytime they or anyone else starts up the computer it will be with Administrator privileges.

This next part cannot be stressed enough. *If you have children in your home, you must set up user accounts for them that do not have Administrator privileges!* Giving someone administrator privileges is essentially giving them the "keys to the kingdom." You can install blocking or filtering software all you like, but if your child has Administrator privileges they can simply uninstall the program whenever they want. In addition, your child would be able to install programs such as BitTorrent, which would allow them to join peer-to-peer networks and download pornography. Here's another tough part: *you can't ask your children for help when setting up your computer!* This "help" would inevitably include them finding out what your password is, which would undo any efforts to restrict their access.

By way of example, let's take a look at Mrs. D. She buys a new Windows-based computer and takes it home. Mrs. D knows a little bit about computers, and her intention is for the machine to be used by her alone. She sets up the computer with a new account, which by default has Administrator privileges. Because she does not want her children using the computer, she sets up a password. Anyone who starts up the computer must type in the password before they can start using it. Mrs. D chooses a password that is based on her favorite television show: "DspHswvs." She is a little forgetful, so she writes the password down on a slip of paper that she sticks in her purse.

A few months go by, and Mrs. D's daughter "E" asks to use the computer for a school project. Mrs. D decides to set up a new account on the computer that does not have Administrator privileges. She follows the instructions and has E select her own password (so brother "F" can't get on by simply starting it under her name). Now when the computer is started up, a screen appears that has 2 different accounts listed: Mrs. D's account, and E's account. Once one account is selected, the appropriate password must be entered to be able to use the computer. If E's account is used, because she does not have Administrator privileges she cannot install or uninstall programs.

At this point, E has no restrictions on the Internet. Another month goes by, and Mrs. D's son F is complaining that E gets to use the computer but he does not. Mrs. D is concerned about F using the computer, because he got into trouble at school for downloading pornography. Mrs. D decides to let F get on the computer, but before she sets up his account she downloads and installs a blocking program, so F cannot use the computer to look for porn.

When setting up his account she does not give him administrator privileges, so he cannot download and install peer-to-peer programs. The blocking program restricts access on both E and F's accounts. Because Mrs. D is the Administrator, she is able to override the program if she wants to. All this works fine, until F roots through Mrs. D's purse one day looking for spare change, and comes across the slip of paper with her password on it. The next time he is alone in the house, he starts up the computer using her account. His first step is to neuter the blocking program by changing the program's options and removing the restrictions against sexual material (which he can do, as the administrator). F goes on a porn binge, downloading as much free material he can and saving it to a USB "thumb drive." F then changes the blocking program's settings back to where they were, clears the browser history, and shuts everything down.

When Mrs. D comes home from work and gets on the computer under her account, she is surprised by a number of pornographic emails that are sent to her. Suspicious, she checks the browser and sees that the history has been cleared out – which she did not do herself. Finally, she looks in the settings to see when someone last started up the computer, and notes that the administrator account had been in use for an hour-long period when she was not at home. It isn't hard to figure out what happened, as F was the only person at home during that time. While he first claims that some freakish "computer glitch" is responsible, F soon fesses up.

This story is used both to demonstrate how individual user accounts are set up, and also to stress the importance of keeping your password secure. We have had cases where the parent had indeed "password protected" their computer, but their child learned very quickly where the password was kept, rendering the whole exercise futile.

Blocking / Filtering Programs

You will recall that in the above story, Mrs. D decided to download and install a program that would restrict her son's Internet access. These programs are commonly referred to as "blocking" or "filtering" programs. They work by prohibiting access to Internet sites that contain inappropriate content. Most of the sites blocked have dealt with pornography, but programs such as NetNanny also have options to block sites that traffic in online gambling, hate speech, or extreme violence. If the program is working properly, it will prevent an individual from navigating to a pornographic web site when they type the site's address in the address window at the top of the browser.

Taking NetNanny for example, if a child attempts to go to the Penthouse website by typing the name in the address window, a message will pop up indicating that the site is restricted due to its sexual content. These programs may also affect search engines like Google. If someone does a Google search for "porn," for example, the list they get will no longer contain any actual pornographic sites. Finally, a good blocking program will also keep someone from navigating to an inappropriate site by clicking on a link that exists on another site. As noted earlier, blocking programs have their options set by the "Administrator" account, and these options can also be changed by that account. So installing a program like NetNanny can be effective, but if you then allow your child to get on the computer using an account with administrator privileges, the child can undo everything you set up.

The use of blocking or filtering programs has created something of a controversy regarding censorship and free speech. The argument is that these programs block a lot more than pornography, and can restrict access to appropriate sites because they have terms that are tangentially related to sexual content. For example, a teenager may be working on a school project about breast cancer, but cannot look up sites dealing with breast cancer because they have the word "breast" in them. In these cases, a good filtering program will have a list of "allowed" sites, which the program will permit access to regardless of their content.

NetNanny allows the user to send a request to the administrator (usually their mother or father) that a particular site be placed on the approved list. The parent can then review the site to determine if it is appropriate for their child or not. If they think it is okay, they can put it on the approved list, and from that point on their child will be able to access it.

Preventing Installation of Unauthorized Programs

In addition to controlling your computer's Internet browser, you need to be able to keep your children from downloading and installing programs without your knowledge. This is because peer-to-peer programs like BitTorrent are freely available, and once downloaded they allow the user to search for pornographic material stored on other privately owned computers on the peer-to-peer network.

Some blocking programs offer an option that supposedly prohibits a user from using peer-to-peer networks. However, in tests we have successfully utilized peer-to-peer networks even on computers that have blocking software enabled. The simplest and most effective solution is to ensure that such programs as BitTorrent are never installed on your computer. This can be accomplished by giving your children user accounts that do not have administrator privileges. This will prevent them from installing anything on their own.

Checking the Browser History

Even if you have taken all the above steps, it pays to periodically check your Internet browser's "history" to see what has been viewed. Checking the history is a little bit different for each browser, but it is usually an easy procedure. For example, on Internet Explorer (the default Windows browser) there is a button near the top of the browser window that allows the user to see all the sites that have been visited over a certain period of time.

The browser has an option that allows you to determine how long the history is maintained – for example you can set it so the browser lists every site that has been viewed in the past month. While this is a good system, there is also a very easy procedure for clearing the browser history manually – and you typically don't need to have administrator privileges to do this. One way of getting around this problem is to make a house rule that clearing the browser history is prohibited, and any time your child clears their history without permission there will be a consequence, such as taking away their computer access for a set period of time. Some blocking software (such as NetNanny) keeps an independent list of all the websites visited over a period of time, and this list cannot be cleared unless the individual has administrator privileges.

Checking the Computer's Hard Drive

In addition to viewing pornography online, your child may have downloaded pornography onto your computer's hard drive. Most people rarely venture into the forbidding jungle that is their computer's filing system. Operating systems tend to give users clearly labeled files ("My Documents," "My Videos," and so on), and that is where they tend to store any files they create or download. A crafty child, however, may bury a pornographic video clip or picture deep in obscure folders or directories. One method for searching for inappropriate files is to use the computer's "Search" function to look for pictures or video clips. There will be a brief instructional guide in the appendix of this book to help you do such a search.

Of course, your child may have deleted any pornographic files they downloaded. However, there does exist a computer program that can look for deleted files: http://undeleteplus.com/. We should note that before you go looking through a computer's files, you should make sure you have a legal right to do so. If you own the computer, there is no conflict. If you want to check your boyfriend or neighbor's computer without their knowledge, however, you could potentially be charged with a crime.

Restricting Internet Access on Game Systems

As noted above, many game systems such as the Wii, PS3, and PSP have Internet browsers. The major problem for parents is that right now, there is no way of putting blocking software on these browsers. However, the Wii, PS3, and PSP do offer parents the option of restricting access to the Internet browser. If the parent elects to take this option, they set up a 4-digit code. Then, whenever someone tries to use the browser they must enter the proper code before they can proceed. When setting up such a code, it may be tempting to make it something very easy for you to remember, such as "0000," or "1234." Be advised that your child is likely to try these codes, and so you should make it something appropriately random.

If your game system offers Internet access, check the manual to see if there is an option to restrict access – this will usually be found in a "parental controls" section. If the manual has no information, check online.

Restricting Internet Access on Cell Phones

Probably the easiest way of controlling content your child may see on their cell phone is to make sure the model they have does not have the ability to access the Internet – Verizon, for example, calls this feature "Mobile Web." If the cell phone does have a web browser, some phone companies offer parental controls in an effort to restrict content the phone's user can access. Both the iPhone and the iPod Touch have a feature that allows a parent to lock out Internet access by using a 4-digit code.

Physical Location of the Computer

One effective way of limiting opportunities for viewing Internet pornography is to have the computer in a well-traveled section of the house. There is a big difference between having the computer in the living room, and having it in the child's bedroom. Sometimes just the risk of being discovered is enough to keep a child from looking for Internet pornography. However, as has been noted earlier in the book, there have been cases of children accessing pornography when their parent or guardian was just a few feet away. Children who are addicted to Internet pornography will be willing to take such risks, so great is their compulsion to view porn.

The One Sure-Fire Method

There is one method that absolutely ensures that your child cannot access Internet pornography without your knowledge, and that is to sit right beside them while they are online. Obviously, this is a time-consuming and intrusive procedure. We typically recommend such a step only if the child has documented sexual issues, and they have to have Internet access for school. If the child has significant sexual issues and does not need to get online for school, there is really no reason to allow *any* Internet access.

How Much is Too Much?

Parents reading this section may wonder how much they need to do to adequately protect their children, and at what point are they unfairly and unnecessarily invading their child's privacy. The balance between privacy and safety is a tricky one, and there is no one-stop answer. It depends on the child, and on their situation. Generally, the more at risk the child is, the more steps should be taken to control their Internet access.

If your child has gotten into trouble multiple times at home and at school for downloading pornography, or if your child has committed a sexual offense, then the strictest measures are clearly warranted. In any event, there really is no reason *not* to take some of the steps listed above, in particular giving your child an account that does not have administrator privileges, and having a good blocking /filtering program installed. These steps take a minimum of effort, and will do much to keep your child from inappropriate material online.

How Children Try to Get Around Efforts to Restrict their Internet Access

One thing we tell parents of the current generation is that their children already know more about computers and the Internet than they themselves will ever know. We're not trying to scare them, but instead want to emphasize that their kids are smart, computer savvy, and in many cases won't take efforts to restrict their access lying down. Some children will try to defeat parental control efforts because they are genuinely obsessed with pornography. Other children will try because they like a challenge. And still more children will try because they don't like the fact that they are being restricted from something. Parents need to be aware of the methods their children may use to circumvent their best efforts. We should note that we first learned about many of the methods listed below not from a book, but from children we were treating for sexual issues.

Circumventors

"Circumventors" are web sites designed to get around blocking and filtering programs. They are a version of what is known as a "proxy server." To understand proxy servers, you need to know a little about how blocking software typically interacts with the Internet browser. Normally, your home computer communicates directly with servers that distribute Internet content (see Figure A).

Figure A – Typical Internet Connection

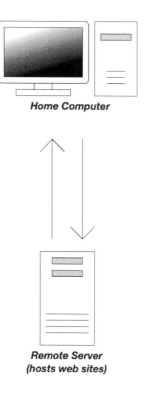

Home Computer

Remote Server
(hosts web sites)

Many blocking programs make use of a proxy server, which is maintained by the blocking program's company. It acts like a gatekeeper, deciding what content from the Internet to allow through to your computer based on the options you selected on the program you have installed at home. If you are using one such blocking program, any time you access the Internet you are first routed through the proxy server (see Figure B).

Figure B – Using a Blocking/Filtering Program

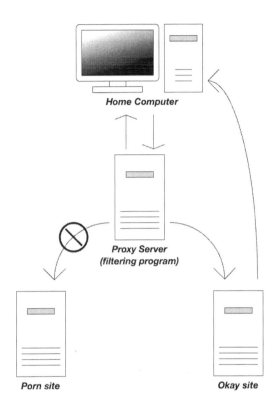

The key is that blocking programs block sites that they believe are inappropriate (because the site has pornographic material, for example), and allow access to sites that do not contain blocked material. A *circumventor* is a site that appears to the blocking program to be harmless, but actually acts as an additional proxy server that will then allow access to pornographic sites (see Figure C). When blocking programs become aware of such sites they put them on their blocked lists, but new ones keep popping up all the time.

Figure C – How a Circumventor Gets Around Filtering Programs

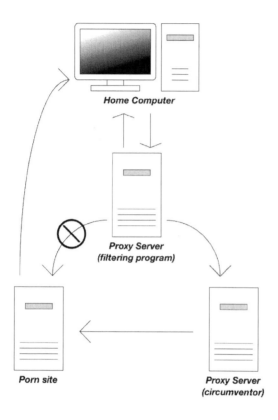

There is actually a web site that is openly dedicated to helping minors get around blocking software. It is called Peacefire,[8] and it was created and is maintained by a man named Bennett Haselton. Among its other services, Peacefire offers to send lists of circumventor sites that have not yet been blocked by filtering programs. Haselton's stated objection to blocking software is that it infringes on free speech and free access to information. While he appears to be aware that his methods help minors get access to pornography, the following quote from his website clearly shows his attitude about this:

If you want to know whether minors can handle a particular right, like the right to read whatever books and watch whatever movies they want, why not just look at how people under 18 handle it already? Can minors handle the responsibility for their own library cards? Why not just ask the ones who already have one? Or, if you had told people 15 years ago that someday there would be a global computer network that kids could use to access ALL THE PORN IN THE WORLD right from their OWN HOUSE, many people would have been horrified. Now that it's been around for 10 years, there's no evidence that it has affected kids' well-being -- so having a "debate" about whether people under 18 can handle being on the Internet, is a bit silly at this point, because we already know that they can.[9]

Such a statement demonstrates what can only be described to us in this field as jaw-dropping ignorance. Using Haselton's argument, one might as well argue that children should be allowed to openly purchase pornography from adult video stores, because obviously they can "handle" it. It should be noted that NetNanny, in addition to blocking pornographic sites, also by default blocks sites that have the keyword "proxy," no doubt to prevent children from gaining access to circumventors. Peacefire is one such blocked site – we're sure Haselton appreciates the irony. However, as of this writing it is still easy to obtain lists of circumventor sites, even if you have blocking software installed. We recently came across a post online by an adolescent girl asking for circumventor sites to get around her school's blocking software – an answering post gave links to no less than 8 such sites.

Misspelling Words

Most web sites have certain terms associated with them, which helps search pages like Google to find them. For example, MTV's site has terms like "music," "videos," and "music videos" associated with it (these terms are called "Meta-Tags"). Thus, when someone types any of those terms in a search engine, the engine will note that MTV is a site that has such content, and will send a link for that site to the person who is doing the searching. Many web pages, wanting as many visitors as possible, have started to include common misspellings of these terms – so those of us who have typed a search term in a hurry and messed it up will still get links to the sites we are looking for. So, you can type in "muisic" instead of "music," and still get plenty of web sites that deal in music.

How does this relate to children getting around Internet blockers? Pornographic sites also include common misspellings of their search terms – misspellings that may not be caught by the blocking software. Some children have learned this, and may try a whole variety of misspelled sexual terms in an effort to find the one term that their blocking software hasn't caught.

Many of the early blocking programs were based on lists of known pornographic web sites, as well as lists of sexual search terms. It was fairly easy to defeat these lists by using misspelled words (a particular program might have had "lesbian" on its blocked list, but wouldn't have "lesbion").The more sophisticated blocking programs get around such limitations by dynamically assessing the content of each individual website that a user tries to access, and then allowing or denying access based on their analysis. With these programs, a child could manage to obtain a link to a pornographic site by use of a misspelled search term, but when the child tries to access the site the blocker would first assess the site's content, and then deny access because of the pornography.

Foreign Languages

Many Americans don't realize that the Internet is a truly international phenomenon, and that there are literally millions of web sites that originate from foreign countries, and which are in a foreign language. Some savvy American children know this, however, because they realized that they could get around their (English language) blocking software by typing search terms not in English, but in Spanish, German, Swedish, or other languages. For example, they could find out the German language equivalent of, say, "anal sex" by going to the library or bookstore and looking through German-English dictionaries. There are also plenty of web sites that offer free translations of words, phrases, or sentences from English to any number of other languages.
As with misspelled words, however, the best blocking software can get around the foreign language loophole by dynamically assessing the content of any site that the child attempts to visit, regardless of what language the site is in.

Social Networking

Many adults can remember their parents admonishing them not to talk to strangers. Undoubtedly one reason our parents didn't want us talking to strangers was the fear that there could be bad people out there who could do us harm. We may have thought our parents were being silly and paranoid, but one look at the nightly news is sufficient evidence that there are indeed bad people out there. The good news is that sexual predators don't hang around playgrounds and swimming pools quite so much. The bad news is that they've simply moved online, which allows them to hunt for and "groom" victims from the comparative safety of their homes. Television shows like "To Catch a Predator" have demonstrated that there are all too many adults who use the Internet to find vulnerable children that they can exploit. It is very important that parents understand how these social networking systems work.

In addition to the danger of being solicited by a predator, social networking is another means by which children are being prematurely sexualized. We have treated children as young as 12 who have engaged in many sexually explicit conversations online, sometimes with adults (men *and* women). Even if the child does not end up making physical contact with the adult, the sexual conversations themselves are potentially harmful. Children are also increasingly engaging in highly sexualized behavior with each other online, which increases the risk that they will engage in sexual behaviors for real – sometimes indiscriminately, without regard for the risks of pregnancy or sexually transmitted diseases.

Chat Rooms

Probably the most prevalent form of online communication other than email is the chat room. A chat room is essentially a "virtual" room where various people online can communicate with each other. The "room" itself exists on whichever computer server is hosting it, and individual computer users can join the group and participate in the discussion. Chat rooms exist for just about every topic under the sun, from politics and social issues to hobbies and particular television shows.

One major host for chat rooms is Yahoo, which has a major section of its website devoted exclusively to online chat. The Yahoo site is illustrative of how easy it is for a child to gain access to adult chat rooms. All you need to do is sign up for a Yahoo account. The sign-up process includes submitting your birthday, but a clever child or adolescent could simply give him or herself a birthday that makes them an "adult." There is no attempt to verify the person's age or identity. Once the adolescent has the account, they can browse through the hundreds of chat rooms available. If they try to look at "adult" chat rooms, they must click a button that says they are 18 or older – they are then given full access. There is a whole subset of chat rooms labeled "adult," and which have topics such as "erotic cartoons," "masturbation," "exhibitionism and voyeurism," "fetishes," and "sex toys."

A major issue with chat rooms is children being solicited by adults to engage in sexual chat. Many children growing up in this day and age have come to see online chat as merely another form of talking to people, and some children and adolescents chat online in an effort to make a connection to someone.

The children most at risk for online solicitation are also those children more likely to chat online – lonely, socially isolated, and estranged from their parents. Online predators are very skilled at luring in such children, and making it seem as if they empathize and understand them. In reality, they are merely pretending to care while they work towards turning the conversation towards sex. Soliciting a child or adolescent into a sexual conversation online is bad enough, but many perpetrators have the goal of meeting the child in person, obviously with the intention of engaging in sex with them.

Web Cams

A fairly common addition to online chat has been the webcam. This is basically an inexpensive video camera that sends a video signal across the Internet. Many new laptop computers have a webcam built in, and some desktop computers have built in webcams (the current model of iMac, for example). If your computer does not have a built in webcam, you can buy one fairly cheaply and install it.

Webcams allow people chatting with each other online to also see each other in real time, and in some settings even hear them. There is a large subset of pornographic web sites that focus on webcams. These sites have a number of women who are online, and who can be seen via their webcam. The sites offer users the opportunity to "chat" with the women and tell them to do sexual things so the user can see.

Webcams cause two additional problems with respect to children. First, children and particularly adolescents may engage in sexual chat with each other. There are plenty of situations where adolescents want to date, but whose parents have forbidden it because they think they are too young to date, or because they do not like the person their child wants to date. Adolescents may choose to pursue the relationship anyway, using online chat and webcams to have a quasi-sexual relationship.

Second, a child who is chatting online with someone using webcams could be bribed, manipulated, or otherwise encouraged to engage in some form of sexual activity, to be viewed through the webcam by the person they are chatting with. A story that appeared on *The New York Times* told of a young boy who had gotten a webcam and began chatting online. He was eventually solicited by many different adult men to perform sexual acts for them via the webcam. The boy was extensively manipulated through gifts and money to do these things. One of the adults went so far as to rent the boy an apartment, so he could engage in such behavior without fear of being disturbed. The boy ended up meeting with at least some of these men and being molested by them.

MySpace and Facebook

Social networking sites have exploded in usage over the past few years. The two most popular sites by far are MySpace and Facebook. As of mid-2008, MySpace had 73 million users in the United States alone, while Facebook had 36 million. A 2007 study by the Pew Internet & American Life

Project[10] found that 55% of online American youths aged 12 to 17 years used online social networking sites. Only 3 years later, that number increased to 73%.[11]

Sites like MySpace and Facebook allow a user to create a customized web page of their own, where they can include personal information, photos, favorite songs, and video clips. Connections are formed with other people on the site by becoming "friends" with them – this allows each to view the other's page. On MySpace, the user determines who can see their profile. They can make their profile "open," meaning anyone can view it, or they can restrict the profile only to those individuals they have invited to become "friends."

On Facebook the user can limit access to friends, or can allow "friends of friends" to view their page as well. You must be at least 13 years old to have a profile on MySpace or Facebook. However, it would be easy for a child 12 or younger to set up a profile – all they have to do is put in a fake birthday. A study done in England in 2008 suggested that there were as many as 750,000 British children who had profiles on social networking sites despite being underage.[12] There are many other social networking sites, and quite a few (such as imeem) have no age restrictions.

As with online chat, the major concern with social networking sites is that sexual predators may use the sites to gain access to children and form relationships with them, potentially leading to a face-to-face meeting. In 2009, a news story reported that MySpace deleted *90,000* profiles, because the users were convicted sex offenders. Keep in mind that those 90,000 were *convicted* sex offenders. There is no way to know how many offenders are online, who have not been caught.

Suggestions for Parents

Parents can learn a lot about their children by looking at their MySpace or Facebook page. The page shows how your child wants to be seen by other people. Naturally, you want to make sure there are no inappropriate pictures or other material on the site. However, it also makes sense to check the sites of your child's "Friends."

In one case a young boy in treatment showed his therapist his MySpace page, and one of his "friends" was an adult woman who had on her site a banner stating that she "f__ked like a porn star." Needless to say, the boy's grandmother made him delete this woman from his friends list. Parents should be suspicious of any "friend" who is an adult they personally do not know.

Another thing parents can do is caution their children against providing too much personal information to people they chat with on the Internet. The following things should *never* be disclosed:

- Their home telephone number
- Their cell phone number
- Their home address
- Their neighborhood location
- The name of their school
- Their popular hangouts

If your child complains that these things are hardly a secret to neighborhood or school friends they chat with, you can answer that if they already know, there is no need to tell them while online.

Sex offenders can be very clever about taking bits of information and using them to determine the physical location of the child they are communicating with. MySpace and

Facebook give users the option of how much personal information to display on their page – the information listed above should never be made available to people who can see the page.

Cell Phones and "Sexting"

A cell phone-facilitated behavior that is on the upswing is "sexting," which is using instant messaging services to send sexually explicit texts, pictures, and videos to people. A survey conducted by TRU[13] in 2008 showed that 20% of the teens surveyed had electronically sent a nude or nearly nude picture or video of themselves. Of teen girls aged 13 through 16, 11% had electronically sent a nude or nearly nude picture or video of themselves.

When the subject turned to sexually suggestive text messages or emails, 39% of all teens surveyed indicated they had sent such messages. In early 2008, a Pennsylvania school was hit by a scandal when 2 girls sent sexually explicit photos and videos of themselves to schoolmates, who then sent the material to others in their phones' address books. As many as 40 children viewed the material before school officials and police intervened. Because the girls involved were underage, anyone receiving the images could have been charged with possession of child pornography, and anyone sending the images could have been charged with distribution. Indeed, in January 2009, an MSNBC story revealed that 3 underage girls were being charged with the manufacture and distribution of child pornography after they took nude or semi-nude pictures of themselves and sent them to boys. The 3 boys who were found to have these images on their phones were being charged with possession of child pornography.[14]

If a cell phone has MMS (Multimedia Message Service) capability, it can send and receive images and video clips through the service. At present most phones have SMS (Short

Message Service) capability only, which means the messages must be text only. However, many cell phone companies offer their users the ability to send pictures taken with the phone's camera to other phones – this service is often referred to as "Picture Mail." We have had adolescent clients who received nude pictures of girlfriends or female acquaintances using such a service.

Some cell phone providers have a means of disabling the phone's camera. You can also pick a cell phone company that allows you to block your child from texting to so-called "short codes," which would prevent them from using text messaging to communicate with pornographic web sites or businesses.

One surefire way of preventing your child from using their cell phone to send inappropriate messages is to not give them a cell phone at all. However, there are many advantages to adolescents having cell phones, not the least being that parents can stay in ongoing communication with their children. While taking the above-mentioned steps can make it difficult for a child to engage in "sexting," the most effective way is likely sitting down with your child and talking to them about why they should not be doing it. There are 3 important reasons why "sexting" is potentially damaging and dangerous behavior, and these reasons should be explained thoroughly to your child:

1. As already mentioned earlier in this chapter, minors who take pictures of themselves nude or semi-nude have just broken the law by manufacturing child pornography. If they send the picture to someone, they have now distributed child pornography. And the person to whom they sent the picture is now guilty of possessing child pornography. Children *have been prosecuted* for these crimes after engaging in "sexting."

2. Many if not most adolescents who engage in sexting probably labor under the belief that if they send a nude picture of themselves to a boyfriend or girlfriend, it will go no further than that. But time after time these pictures have been sent on to many others – it only takes one person with a vindictive nature to send a single picture to every phone number they can think of. Your daughter may think her boyfriend is the love of her life and would never do such a thing, but that could change quickly if they break up. In one nationally known case, a 13-year-old girl had sent a nude picture of herself to a boy she liked. The picture was circulated to a large number of children at their school. The girl endured vicious taunting as a result, and eventually committed suicide.[15]

3. Many cases of "sexting" involve adolescent girls sending nude pictures of themselves to their boyfriends or male acquaintances. There are undoubtedly many reasons why these girls engage in this behavior – to feel sexy, to gain attention, or even as a joke. They need to consider, however, what message the recipient will take from the image. A boyfriend who receives such an image may assume that the girl wants to have sex with him, when her intention may have been far different. Certainly this is no excuse for the boy to coerce the girl into a sexual encounter. But adolescents need to consider how their actions are going to be viewed by others.

There is one theme that runs through each of these 3 points, and it should be reinforced again and again to your child - it only takes a second to take a nude picture of yourself and send it, but the consequences could easily last for a very long time.

Conclusion

It is easy for parents to feel overwhelmed when facing the task of trying to protect their children from the darker side of the Internet age. Technology has made it increasingly easy for a child to place him or herself in a potentially dangerous situation, or to see things no child was ever meant to see. There are companies and organizations dedicated to protecting children that are trying to keep up, but the funding for their work pales in comparison to the money that can be made by making access to pornography quicker and simpler.

There are also people who claim that the alarm over Internet pornography, and the risks posed to children, is unreasonable and unnecessary. A typical argument is that American culture is still repressed when it comes to sexuality, and the outcry over such things as "sexting" and access to pornography is due to a hysterical fear of normal childhood sexuality. Some authors also feel that we don't give children enough credit for knowing what is safe behavior online.

We have no doubt that there are children and adolescents who have good sense when it comes to their online activities and behavior. It's very likely, however, that those children came by that good sense because they had parents who cared enough to set limits and form clear expectations for their children's behavior. The most important step a parent can take to protect their child is to do their best to create a warm, honest, and candid relationship with the child. Remember, though, that part of creating that relationship includes working to understand the child's world – including the Internet, instant messaging, and social networking. After all, you can't talk to your child unless you understand the language they are speaking.

Keeping Your Kids Away from Pornography

☐ Keep any pornography in your home in a locked cabinet that your child cannot access

☐ Keep computers or televisions in public areas rather than in your child's bedroom, basement, or other private areas of the home

☐ Put parental controls on all of the televisions, computers, and other Internet-accessible devices such as cell phones, videogame systems, and PDAs

☐ Use parental controls to block access to pay-per-view movies and movie channels.

☐ Do not allow DVD players or VCRs in your child's bedroom.

☐ Make sure your child does not have administrator privileges on your computers

☐ Make sure your child does not know your password

☐ Regularly check the browser history on all home computers

☐ Do not allow your child to spend time unsupervised in places where there are no parental controls on TVs, computers, or Internet-accessible devices

---

[1] Retrieved from enough.org, based on a 2006 Internet Filter Review
[2] Ibid
[3] www.familysafemedia.com/pornography_statistics.html
[4] "For X-Rated, a Domain of Their Own," by Miguel Helft; published on www.nytimes.com on 6/25/10
[5] American Library Association website, retrieved 1/2010

[6] News story reported by Brad Hawkins for WFAA-TV on 1/15/2008

[7] www.wififreespot.com

[8] www.peacefire.org

[9] Ibid

[10] Lenhart, A. & Madden, M. (2007). Social networking sites and teens. Pew Internet & American Life Project, http://pewinternet.org/~media//Files/ Reports/2007/ PIP_SNS_Data-Memo_Jan_2007.pdf.pdf

[11] Zickuhr, K. (2010). Generations 2010. Pew Internet & American Life Project, http://www.pewinternet.org/~/media// Files/ Reports/ 2010/PIP_Generations_and_Tech10.pdf

[12] "Facebook: Children evade social websites' age limits," by John Carvel; published on www.guardian.co.uk on 7/8/2008

[13] "Sex and Tech: Results from a Survey of Teens and Young Adults," Published by the National Campaign to Prevent Teen and Unwanted Pregnancy

[14] "Sexting surprise: Teens face child porn charges," by Mike Brunker; published on www.msnbc.msn.com on 1/15/09

[15] "Sexting-related bullying cited in Hillsborough Teen's Suicide," by Andrew Meacham; published by St. Petersburg Times on 11/29/09

Chapter 8: What To Do If Your Child Shows Sexual Behaviors

Introduction

Mrs. J had been having a pretty calm time of it so far, considering it wasn't a school day. Fortunately her 9-year-old son, David, was outside playing with his best friend, Seth, which left her relatively free to get started on her many household chores. She had just finished washing the dishes and was putting them away when she happened to glance out the window into the backyard. What she saw paralyzed her, a coffee cup grasped in one frozen hand. Seth was on all fours, and David was kneeling behind him. For an instant Mrs. J thought they were playing leapfrog, until she realized to her shock that both had their pants pulled down. David was moving up to Seth's bottom when Mrs. J found her voice and started yelling at them to stop. The boys jumped, looked back at the house, and scrambled to pull their pants up. Mrs. J felt stunned and angry. She never would have believed that David could do such a thing. As David and Seth trudged shame-facedly towards the kitchen door, Mrs. J kept asking herself one question: What on earth do I do now?

Like Mrs. J, many parents feel very upset when they find their children showing sexual behavior. Some parents are quick to punish the child, and they may tell the child that such behavior is wrong or "nasty." Other parents spank the child, as they would to punish any misbehavior. While this is a gut instinct for many parents, it is not a good idea. Punishing the child teaches the child that sexual behaviors are bad, which could result in the child having sexual hang-ups as an adult.

This also teaches the child to be more secretive about their sexual behaviors in order to avoid being punished. Even worse, this can shut down the parent's communication with the child, as the child may think he or she will get in trouble for talking about any sexual issues. As a parent, you want your child to feel safe and comfortable talking to you about sexual issues. This is especially important so that you can find out where and how your child learned their sexual behaviors. If your child worries about being punished, he or she is much less likely to tell you if they have been sexually abused or exposed to pornography. It may also be that your child is just displaying normal curiosity for his or her age, and that there is nothing to be worried about. Your job as the parent is to get more information from your child so you can determine if there is a problem.

What is the Best Way to Respond to Your Child's Sexual Behaviors?

If you catch your child engaging in sexual behaviors, it is best to stay calm and ask the child or children what they are doing. For example, if you catch your child on top of another child making humping motions, you could calmly ask, "what are you doing?" You should then separate the children in different rooms and calmly ask each child separately and privately what happened. Your job is to find out as many details as you can about what happened, whose idea it was to engage in the sexual activity, and how they got the idea to engage in such behavior. We recommend that you *first* talk to the youngest child or the child that you think probably did not initiate the sexual activity. The reason for this is that the child who initiated the sexual activity is less likely to tell the truth, as he or she may be worried about getting in trouble, particularly if the child knows that he or she did something wrong. Children who act out sexually often blame the other child, claiming that the other child initiated the sexual talk or sexual play. This can make it very confusing for parents, as they are unsure which child to believe.

Here is a list of potential questions you could ask each child separately:

"Tell me what happened."
- Ideally, you want the child to tell you in their own words what happened, with as little prompting as possible. However, most children in this situation tend to "clam up." If this happens, be sure to give the child plenty of time to respond to your question before asking another question. It may also help to calmly reassure the child that you just want them to tell the truth so you can understand what happened.

- Have the child describe in as much detail as possible what happened leading up to the event. For example, if you found them in the bedroom, you could ask, "How did you end up in the bedroom? Whose idea was it to come in the bedroom? What did you do once you got in the bedroom? What happened after that?" Ask the child to describe all of the events that occurred leading up to your discovery of the sexual activity.

"Did you and ___ (other child's name) do this before? How many times?"
"How did you or ___ (the other child) get the idea to do this?"
"How did you feel about this?"
"What did ___ (the other child) say to you?"
"What did you say to them?"

Make sure that you reassure the child that he or she is not in trouble, and you just want to understand what happened.

If one child is 3 or more years younger than the other child, then ask the older child:

> *"How did you get _____ (the younger child) to go along with it?"*
> *"What did you say to _____ (the younger child)?"*
> *"Did you tell ___ (the younger child) that you would give him/her something like a toy?"*
> *"Did you tell him/her to not tell?"*

If you strongly believe in spanking the child for sexual behavior that is clearly abusive (such as a teen performing anal sex on a 5-year-old), then make sure that you ONLY spank the older child. Do not spank the younger child, as the younger child is the victim. Unfortunately, we have encountered a lot of parents who automatically spank both children involved, with no regard for which child is actually responsible. Spanking both children sends the message that the victim shares the blame for the sexual abuse. This can result in the victim feeling guilty and responsible for the victimization. This also encourages the abuser to place blame on the victim, which then allows the abuser to justify his sexual acting out. These distorted beliefs can make it hard for both parties to heal after the sexual abuse, and they increase the risk of the sexual abuse occurring again.

As the parent, you may need to remind yourself that the blame rests entirely with the abuser, and that the victim is not to blame. Even if the younger child seems to be highly sexualized, you should not assume that the younger child initiated the sexual activity. It may be that the younger child is sexualized *because* he or she has been sexually abused. Older children, particularly those who molest, tend to be savvy about hiding their sexual behaviors while younger children are not. That can result in the adult getting the impression that the younger child is the initiator of the sexual activity when in fact the older child has simply just been better at hiding his sexual behavior.

Is the Sexual Behavior Normal?

Before you react to your child's sexual behaviors, consider whether or not the sexual behavior is normal for your child's age. See Chapter 2 for more information about what is considered normal. You should consider the following:

- Your child's age and the age of the other child involved
- If the sexual contact was consensual
- The types of sexual behaviors that occurred
- How many times this behavior has occurred
- If your child has been caught before for sexual behaviors and told to not repeat such behaviors

---

Is It Considered Sexual Abuse?

Check if any of the following apply:
- ☐ One child is 3 or more years older than the other child
- ☐ One child has significantly more power or knowledge than the other child due to:
    - a prior history of sexual abuse or exposure to pornography
    - an intellectual difference (one child is significantly smarter than the other child)
    - a physical size difference (one child is physically much larger or stronger than the other child)
    - a difference in social power (one child is the leader while the other is a follower)
- ☐ Use of bribes or threats
- ☐ Use of manipulation
- ☐ Use of physical force

If any of these items have been checked, then the sexual activity is probably *not* consensual and it is considered inappropriate, if not abusive.

When Should You Take Further Action?

If there is a 3 year age difference or more between the children, or the sexual contact was abusive (use of threats, bribes, force, or manipulation), then you should immediately report the sexual behavior to your local Child Protective Services or local law enforcement. Child Protective Services (CPS) varies from state to state in how they handle child-on-child sexual abuse cases. CPS often screens out such cases, meaning that they do not investigate such cases. If that is the situation, then you could notify your local law enforcement agency such as the Sheriff's Department.

In all cases, you should tell the parent(s) of the other child who was involved in the sexual activity. This allows that parent to question their child further and seek treatment if needed. Unfortunately, many parents do not seek treatment when needed, even in cases where their child has been sexually abused or has sexually abused another child. Thus, it is important to report any clearly sexually abusive behaviors to CPS or law enforcement, as these agencies can take steps to ensure that the abuser and victim get specialized treatment.

If your child has been sexually abused by a teen or adult, then you should take your child for a physical exam and forensic interview as soon as possible. It is best for this physical exam and interview to be conducted by specialists who are trained to examine children in sexual abuse cases. If you report the abuse to law enforcement or CPS, they may refer you to a Child Advocacy Center (CAC) where such physical exams and/or forensic interviews are typically offered free of charge. In our experience, CACs often will not interview children under age 4, and they only interview children in cases that are referred by law enforcement. In addition, law enforcement and CPS often are reluctant to become involved in cases that involve a pending divorce or custody dispute. Therefore, in those cases, you may need to find a private psychologist or other mental health professional who specializes in sexual issues in children and can evaluate and treat your child. To find such a provider, we recommend that you contact the Safer Society at www.safersociety.org or Prevent Child Abuse America at www.preventchildabuse.org for a referral to a specialist in your area.

Evaluation and Treatment for Your Child

When children are showing inappropriate or excessive sexual behaviors and/or there are concerns of possible sexual abuse, we recommend that the child receive a specialized evaluation that focuses specifically on sexual issues. These evaluations are often called psychosexual or sexual trauma evaluations, although the name may vary depending upon the agency conducting the evaluation. A psychosexual evaluation is the name of the evaluation for a child who is acting out sexually, meaning the child is showing excessive or inappropriate sexual behaviors. A sexual trauma evaluation is the name of the evaluation of a child who may have been sexually abused or is known to have been sexually abused, but the child is not acting out sexually. Both evaluations help assess the child's sexual history, sexual issues, general psychological functioning, and need for treatment. These evaluations should be conducted by a mental health professional with at least a master's degree who has specialized training in assessing sexual issues in children.

How are these evaluations conducted? The evaluator first interviews the parent or caretaker and then interviews the child separately. The parent completes questionnaires about the child's behavior, and these ratings are compared to the ratings by other parents of similar aged children. Older children who can read are also asked to complete questionnaires. The test results help the evaluator determine if the child's behaviors and symptoms are atypical for their age, and if they rise to the level of a clinical problem. For example, many children have problems paying attention at times, but only a handful of children have such severe attention problems that they would be diagnosed with Attention-Deficit/Hyperactivity Disorder. The same is true for sexual behaviors. Most children show some sexualized behaviors, but these behaviors are not considered to be a problem unless they are excessive, inappropriate for the child's age, and/or abusive in nature.

Specialized evaluations can help determine:

- If the child has a sexual problem
- How severe the sexual problem is
- How the child developed the sexual problem
- If the child has significant emotional or behavioral problems
- How the child has responded to any sexual abuse they may have experienced
- If the child needs specialized treatment, and if so, what type of treatment

If an evaluation determines that your child needs treatment, then it is important to follow up and make sure your child receives the needed treatment. Such treatment should help the child cope with any sexual abuse he has experienced, and learn to control any sexual behavior problems. Successful completion of treatment should also help reduce the chance that the child will have sexual problems later in life.

Coping with Your Child's Sexual Behavior Problems

When parents first learn of their child's sexually abusive behavior, they may go through various emotional stages, similar to the stages people experience in response to a death or other trauma. Some parents may go through these stages in order while others may skip certain stages or experience more than one stage at once. Parents can also get stuck at any one stage and remain in that stage. Here are the 5 stages:

Denial:

It is difficult for most parents to believe that their child has a sexual problem. Some parents may not want to believe this because they feel like this reflects negatively on them as parents. They may feel like they have failed as parents, or they may feel guilty that their own actions have resulted in their child developing sexual problems. For example, some parents may know that they were not careful enough about hiding their pornography or sexual activity. Other parents may feel guilty because they know their own alcohol and/or drug use resulted in them being overly lax in supervising their children and may have resulted in their children being exposed to inappropriate situations or people.

Other parents may deny their child's sexual behavior problems, not due to any guilt, but because they simply do not believe their children displayed such behavior. The denial can be so strong that they may hold onto this denial even after their child is convicted of a sex offense in court. It is important to keep in mind that denial among parents is common and to be expected. What is most important, though, is how the parent copes with the denial over time. The goal is for the parent to emerge from the denial so he or she can help the child work on his sexual problem.

Parents vary in how they express their denial. Some parents completely discount any reports that their child is showing sexual behaviors. For example, if the school staff reported the sexual acting out, then the parent may think that the school staff is either lying or exaggerating the behavior. If there is another child involved in the sexual incident, the parents may blame that child and assume that that child is lying or exaggerating the events. For example, they may say things to challenge the other child's credibility by making comments such as, "He's always telling stories" or "She just wanted to get my son in trouble because she doesn't like him." Parents may also blame the other child for being overly sexualized, saying things like, "she's always wearing short skirts" or "she's fast."

Some parents acknowledge their child's sexual behavior, but minimize the inappropriateness of the behavior. For example, they may say things like, "Boys will be boys" or "All kids these days are doing stuff like this." Other parents may minimize by laughing about the behavior, saying things like, "he's my little man" or "he's just like his dad, already a ladies' man." Some parents who had their own sexual issues as a child may think or say, "I did that when I was a kid," implying that their child's behavior is not really a problem.

While denial may be a knee-jerk reaction to a sexual problem, denial can also exist as a creeping paralysis on a parent's response to the problem. The best time to react to the discovery of a serious sexual behavior problem is *immediately*, when the problem is first discovered. Emotions may be high, but motivation to act should also be high. If a parent chooses to wait, to "let things settle down," or "not rush into things," it is very easy to begin coming up with reasons to not take *any* action. Consider the case of Mr. and Mrs. B:

> *Mr. and Mrs. B were initially stunned to hear that their daughter Pam had sexually abused the 6-year-old girl she had been babysitting. They met with the parents of the younger girl, and all agreed that the answer was to get Pam some help. Mr. and Mrs. B promised the victim's parents that they would pursue the matter vigorously. They began looking at therapists, but each was unsuitable for one reason or another. As time went on, Mr. and Mrs. B became less enthused at the prospect of getting their daughter into treatment. After all, Pam had promised she would never do anything like that again, and had stopped babysitting for the time being. Mr. and Mrs. B began to cling to Pam's various excuses – that the touching was merely "curiosity," and had "only" happened once – as reasons why treatment was not really necessary after all. After a year, they even felt comfortable with Pam babysitting again. Thanks in part to their procrastination, Mr. and Mrs. B were able to convince themselves that Pam did not actually have a sexual problem.*

Unfortunately, a lot of parents remain in the denial stage such that they never really acknowledge that their child has a sexual problem. While the parents may think that they are protecting their children, they may in fact be harming their children, as they teach their children to use denial to cope with problems and they are less likely to get professional help for their children. They are doing a disservice to their children, particularly since most children who act out sexually can successfully stop such behaviors if they get counseling and their parents respond appropriately.

Anger:

Many parents who are in the denial stage are also in the anger stage. In this stage, the parents typically direct their anger toward others who they feel are raising the sexual concerns about their child. For example, the parents may be angry with the other child or adult who accused their child of the sexual behaviors. The parents may feel that their child has been targeted unfairly. For example, some parents accuse the school staff of making up such allegations as a way to get their child kicked out of their school. Parents may also become angry with those who try to get help for the child, such as CPS caseworkers, teachers, or counselors. Some of these parents may resent that they are being questioned about their family history and home environment. They may worry that an investigation may uncover some of their own issues such as a family history of sexual abuse, pornography in the house, or poor boundaries such that the children are exposed to sexual material or sexual activity.

Although most parents tend to be angry with others outside of the family during this stage, they may also be angry with their own child for engaging in such behaviors. The parents may feel angry that the child's behavior has resulted in CPS or other agencies becoming involved in their lives. The parents may also feel angry about having to take the child to counseling to address the problem, as this typically requires the parent to take time off from work to drive the child to the appointments and to pay for the therapy sessions.

Parents may also feel angry with themselves, as they may feel that they could or should have done things to prevent their child from developing sexual problems. For example, they may blame themselves for having allowed their child to be around a child molester. Or they may blame themselves for not noticing the signs earlier that their child was being sexually abused. Or they may blame themselves for allowing their child to visit a home where their child was exposed to sexual activity or sexual material. Regardless of who or what is the target of the anger, the anger is usually related to the parent feeling upset that their child now has sexual problems that must be dealt with.

Bargaining :

In this stage, the parent tries to bargain with himself or others in the hopes that they can somehow gain control of the situation. For example, they may bargain with God, saying, "I will be a good mother if you just keep my son from touching his sister again." In other cases parents may plead with the victim's parents to keep them from reporting the abuse, or try to persuade them to drop the charges. The parent often feels desperate and looks for some way to feel in control.

Depression:

In this stage, parents feel depressed, as they realize that their child has a sexual problem. They may feel hopeless and powerless to change the situation, while also believing that the child is irredeemable and incapable of change. They may also blame themselves for their child's problems and view themselves as a bad parent. They may turn to drugs or alcohol to self-medicate their depression and try to forget their problems. They may also give up on trying to supervise their child or follow a safety plan, as this requires constant attention and energy on their part.

Acceptance:

This is the stage that parents will hopefully achieve. In this stage, the parents accept that their child has a sexual behavior problem and they are willing and able to take the necessary steps to deal with the problem. This means that the parents make sure that the child receives counseling and the parents follow a safety plan to make it less likely that the child has the opportunity to act out sexually. Rather than feel depressed, parents in this stage feel empowered as they takes active steps to help their child.

Implementing a Safety Plan

If your child has sexually abused a younger child, then you should implement a safety plan. This plan is designed to help make it less likely that your child will have opportunities to act out sexually again. A safety plan typically involves the following guidelines:

- Avoid leaving your child alone with much younger or more vulnerable children. By more vulnerable, we mean children who are more easily victimized due to intellectual or physical limitations such as a child who has mental retardation or a physical disability. You should provide "eyes on" supervision at all times when your child is with a child who is 3 or more years younger than your child, who is vulnerable, or who was victimized by your child before. This means that you should be in the room and watching your child at all times when your child is around such children. You can have another adult provide this supervision, but this adult should know about your child's sexual acting out and the need for "eyes on" supervision at all times. It can be tempting for you to leave the room briefly, but you really should not do this unless another supervisor is watching your child, as sexual acting out can occur in a matter of seconds.

- Discourage your child from playing with children who are 3 or more years younger. In general, it is better for your child to play with children his or her own age, as this will help improve their social skills and help him or her relate better to peers at school. It will also make it easier for you, as providing "eyes on" supervision for long periods is very demanding and difficult to do.

- Make sure that your child is never placed in a position of authority over younger children or vulnerable children. This means that your child should not be allowed to babysit or act as a "helper" with younger children. Children who act out sexually often offer to help take care of younger children, as this is a way for them to gain access to younger children.

- Make sure that your child sleeps in a bed by himself. Your child should not share a bedroom with younger children or more vulnerable children, or any children with whom he or she has acted out sexually.

- Make sure that your child has no access to younger children during the night. If there is a much younger or vulnerable child in your home, then we recommend that you install an alarm on your child's bedroom door so that you can be alerted at night if your child leaves his room. This is recommended since sexual acting out often occurs at night while the parents are asleep and are therefore unable to supervise their children.

- Make sure that your child takes a bath by herself, with no other children present in the bathroom.

- Teach your child about good boundaries and maintain good boundaries in the home. For example:
  - ➤ Bathrooms and bedrooms are private. Knock first and don't enter unless given permission.
  - ➤ Close doors when someone is changing or using the bathroom.
  - ➤ Everyone should wear adequate clothing around the house. There should be no nudity outside of the bathroom or bedroom.
  - ➤ Bedroom doors should be locked when adults are engaging in sexual activity so children are not exposed to the sexual activity.

- Make sure that your child has no access to

pornography of any kind. Also make sure that your
child has no access to sexually explicit TV shows,
videos, or materials on the Internet. See Chapter 7 for
detailed advice about how to prevent your child's
exposure to pornography.

- Discourage your child from playing games that your
child used to get others to be sexual such as Simon
Says, Doctor, wrestling, Hide-and-Go Seek, Truth or
Dare.

- Avoid putting your child in situations where he or she
is grouped with much younger children or will have
access to much younger children. If your child is in
such a situation, then be sure to notify the staff or
parents (such as at daycare, school, camp, clubs,
parties, swimming classes, etc.) so they can provide the
needed supervision.

Helping Your Child Develop Positive Behaviors

In addition to following a safety plan, you should:

1) **Help your child learn to express feelings in a healthy
way.**

- Encourage your child to talk about his feelings and
listen to what he says. Compliment him when he is
able to talk about his feelings in an appropriate way.

- Explain to your child that it is okay to talk about both
positive and negative feelings, and allow your child to
share his negative feelings. For example, you can
explain that everyone feels angry at times and it is okay
to be angry. However, it is not okay for people to
express their anger in ways that harm others such as by
hitting or kicking.

- Avoid dismissing your child's negative feelings by telling him not to worry or that everything will be okay. Instead, if your child is worried or upset, try to help your child find healthy ways to cope with these feelings.

2) Discourage your child from behaving in controlling or bossy ways.

- Children who act out sexually often have a strong desire to be in control and to control others. Their sexual acting out is often one way that they try to assume control, but they may also try to gain control in nonsexual ways such as by being bossy or controlling with others. Interrupt these behaviors when you see them, and help your child see the negative consequences of such behavior, such as their friends not wanting to play with them anymore.

- Make it clear to your child that it is not okay for him to emotionally or physically hurt others.

- Help your child find healthy and socially acceptable ways to meet his desire for control and attention. For example, you could encourage your child to participate in sports or other structured activities where your child could channel his desire for control in a positive direction, such as by being a team leader.

- Help your child understand that he does not always have to be the best, the first, or have the most of something. Also encourage your child to feel good about what he has and what he is able to accomplish. Avoid comparing your child to others and pointing out his weaknesses or shortcomings.

3) Challenge your child's unhealthy thinking.

- Encourage your child to take responsibility for his behavior instead of blaming his behavior on others. For example, if your child says, "she asked for it" or "she made me do it," point out that only he controls his behavior.

- Discourage your child from viewing himself as a "victim." For example, if he repeatedly blames the teachers at school for getting him in trouble, point out that it is *his* behavior that got him in trouble. As the parent, you should also avoid blaming your child's problems on others, as that will only encourage your child to do the same and avoid taking responsibility for his behavior.

- Remind your child how others are affected by his behaviors. For example, if your child is focusing on the new restrictions he has as a result of his sexual acting out, point out how his sexual acting out has affected others. You want to encourage your child to think about others' feelings and perspectives, not just his own.

What To Do If Your Child Acts Out Sexually Again

If your child acts out sexually again, you should:

- Stay calm.

- If you catch your child in the act, calmly stop the behavior, state why it is not okay, and help your child figure out how he can stop it or control it. Stay with your child to provide needed supervision and to decrease the chance of further acting out.

- Encourage your child to tell you what happened.

- Encourage your child to come to you in the future when he has thoughts of acting out sexually, so you can help him control himself.

- Let your child's therapist know about any sexual acting out so the therapist can address this in the therapy sessions. If your child is not yet receiving specialized treatment for sexual issues, then seek such treatment immediately.

Conclusion

If your child shows sexual behaviors, your response can go a long way towards ensuring that such behaviors are handled appropriately. Reacting calmly to the discovery will likely result in getting more information about what happened and why, which will also allow you to choose the best long-term strategy for dealing with the problem. If your child does have a significant sexual behavior problem, acknowledging the existence of the problem and taking positive steps to treat it will go a long way towards effectively managing the problem and preventing it from getting worse.

Chapter 9: *What To Do If Your Child Discloses Sexual Abuse*

Introduction

No one expects their child to tell them that they have been sexually abused. And most parents have no idea how they would respond if their child did tell them this. This chapter will help you prepare for this moment, should it occur. It is very important that you respond to such a disclosure in an appropriate way. This is for three major reasons. First, how you respond to a disclosure can significantly affect your child's emotional well-being. What you say to your child in that moment could have a huge impact on how your child feels about the abuse and feels about you. Second, how you respond can determine whether or not your child "shuts down" after the first few sentences or gives you details about all that has happened to her. And third, if you end up going to court as a result of the disclosure, how you initially responded to the disclosure can become a big issue in court.

Steps to Take if Your Child Says Something that Suggests Possible Sexual Abuse

Many children, especially young children, disclose sexual abuse by making a comment out of the blue, such as "my tee tee hurts." Or they may ask a question such as, "Why does Uncle Joe have hair on his weenie?" It is very important that you respond to such statements appropriately so that you have the best chance of finding out what has happened. Here is what we recommend:

1)   **First and foremost, you should stay calm.**

This is a tall order for most parents, as the natural reaction is to get upset that your child may have been abused or that your child is accusing a loved one of abusing them. Many children are afraid to tell about abuse because they worry that their parents will be angry with them and will get very upset. If you become very upset, your child may withdraw and not tell you any more information. Remember that children tend to believe that anything that goes on around them is *about* them. Thus, if you get angry when your child tells you she was abused, she will likely assume that you are angry with her, even if you are really angry with the perpetrator. Your child may then clam up, for fear of causing any more anger.

Whatever you do, you need to stay calm and control your emotions. You need to show your child that you can emotionally handle whatever she has to tell you, that you are concerned, and that you want to hear what happened. If you do not feel comfortable questioning your child or don't feel you are emotionally able to handle it, then you can take your child to a mental health professional who specializes in evaluating children who are suspected of having been sexually abused (see the section later in this chapter called *The Role of Medical and Mental Health Providers*).

2)   **Talk to your child privately, away from others.**

You want your child to feel as comfortable and safe as possible. Therefore, you should not question the child with the alleged perpetrator in the house or nearby, as the child may not feel safe telling you about the abuse. You should also avoid talking to your child about the abuse within earshot of others, as your child may not feel comfortable telling you such private information when others can hear. Most children feel ashamed of any sexual abuse they have experienced, and they usually have a very hard time talking about it.

3)   **Allow your child to tell you as much as he or she can with as little prompting from you as possible.**

In other words, ask as few questions as possible. It is best to let your child tell you what happened in her own words, and to not assume what may have happened.

4)   **Follow the child's lead.**

For example, if the child tells you, "my tee tee hurts," and the child does not say anything else, then you could simply repeat the child's statement as a question, "your tee tee hurts?" Most children will offer more information at that point. If they don't, then you could say, "tell me about that" or "how does your tee tee hurt?"

5)   **Be sure to use the child's terms rather than adult terms.**

For example, if the child uses words like "tee tee" or "hunching," then you should use those words when asking more about what happened. Avoid introducing any new terms at this point such as "vagina," "penis," or "sex."

6)   Avoid asking questions that suggest an answer.

For example, do *not* ask things such as: "Somebody touched you, didn't they?" Questions like this are considered to be leading questions, meaning that they are leading the child to give a certain answer. When you ask leading questions, the child may just tell you whatever answer he thinks you want to hear. This then makes it difficult to figure out what the truth is. It is also makes it less likely that the case could ever be successfully prosecuted if abuse did in fact occur. You should also avoid asking about specific sexual acts that the child has not mentioned, such as "did he put his private in your private?" In general, it is best to leave the detailed questioning to a professional who is trained in interviewing children about sexual abuse.

7)   Avoid saying things that may cause the child to stop telling you about what happened.

For example, you should avoid saying anything to the child that suggests you do not believe what he is saying such as "No, Uncle Tommy would never hurt you." You should also avoid telling your child about the possible consequences of a disclosure such as "if your dad did that then I would have to leave him" or "he's going to jail." The child may stop offering information as soon as the child realizes the potential negative consequences of making a disclosure.

8)   Pay attention to your child's body language when your child is telling you about the abuse.

Is your child making sexual gestures while telling you what happened? Is your child pacing around the room and twisting her hair, suggesting that she feels anxious? Most children feel some anxiety when telling about sexual abuse, unless they are young and have no idea that the sexual activity was inappropriate. If your child does not know that the behavior was inappropriate, do not immediately communicate that. For example, avoid saying things like, "he shouldn't have done that" or "he is a bad man." It is best to first get all of the information before sharing any of your own thoughts or judgments with the child. Once the child realizes that the behavior was wrong, the child may stop talking and offering information, especially if the child is protective of the abuser and does not want the abuser to get in trouble.

9)   **Pay attention to *your own* body language and expression while talking to your child.**

If you look angry or distraught, your child may decide to stop talking – or even change her story – because she may find your demeanor upsetting. Adopt an "open" posture. If you lean back and fold your arms, you give the impression that you don't want to hear what the child is saying, as in the photo below:

Body language that discourages disclosure

In contrast, if you lean forward, make eye contact, remain calm, and get closer to the child's eye level, the child is more likely to feel comfortable talking to you.

Body language that encourages disclosure

10)   Reassure your child that she did the right thing by telling and that she is not in trouble.

For example, you could say, "I'm glad that you told me" or "That was good to tell." Keep in mind that most sexually abused children are very worried that they will get in trouble for the abuse. Reassure your child that you still love her.

11)   Let your child know that she can talk to you about this any time.

Although it is tempting, do not make promises you may not be able to keep such as saying you won't tell anyone about the abuse.

12)   **Write down your child's statements as soon as possible.**

It is best if you can write down the child's statements without the child seeing. If your child sees you writing while talking, she may become nervous and stop talking. Also write down the context in which your child made the statement and what you asked your child. Ideally, you should try to write down the entire dialogue, including your questions and your child's responses.

13)   **If you are unsure if your child has described abuse or you want immediate help from a professional, you can call the Childhelp USA Hotline at 1-800-4-A-CHILD or go to www.childhelp.org.**

Trained counselors are available 24 hours a day at Childhelp for crisis intervention and referrals to counseling agencies and support groups.

14)   **If you believe your child has described sexual abuse, then you should contact the local authorities.**

Call your local Child Protective Services or Police/Sheriff's Department to report the allegations. States differ in terms of their procedure for reporting alleged abuse. To find out where and how to report child abuse in your state, go to the website for the Child Welfare Information Gateway: www.childwelfare.gov.

15)   **Find a medical doctor and counselor who specialize in evaluating and treating sexual abuse**.

Child Protective Services or law enforcement should help connect you with the appropriate mental health and medical resources to have your child interviewed and physically examined. If these agencies do not respond immediately or are not aware of such resources, then you should look for a medical provider who has experience in conducting physical exams in cases of suspected sexual abuse. You should also contact a local mental health provider who has experience in conducting forensic interviews of children in cases of alleged sexual abuse. The medical and mental health provider is required to report the allegations to law enforcement or Child Protective Services. For help in finding resources in your area, you can all the National Center for Victim of Crime at **1-800-FYI-CALL or 1-800-211-7996. They have a** database of over 10,000 organizations that link victims with a variety of important services such as crisis intervention, assistance throughout the criminal justice process, counseling, support groups and legal counsel.

The Role of Medical and Mental Health Providers

Once your child has said or done things that suggest that sexual abuse has occurred, you need to take your child to a professional who specializes in sexual abuse. That professional can then help you decide which steps to take from that point on. If the child appears to have some bodily signs of sexual abuse such as vaginal redness or genital pain, take your child to the doctor as soon as possible. You should not wait since any physical signs of sexual abuse may go away quickly. If your child has been sexually abused, then it will be very helpful if medical records show that you took your child to the doctor as soon as you were concerned. If the case ever goes to court, the medical records may be very helpful if they show physical evidence or signs of sexual abuse. However, you should know that physical evidence is actually rare in sexual abuse cases. If you take your child to a pediatrician, and the pediatrician does not find any physical evidence of sexual abuse, this *does not mean* that no sexual abuse took place. Remember that many sexual offenses take the form of fondling, which typically does not result in any bruising or other physical signs of abuse. In addition, there is often no physical evidence even where there is vaginal or anal penetration. See "Physical Evidence in Sexual Abuse Cases" later in this chapter for more information.

In addition to a medical exam, you should have your child receive a videotaped, forensic interview by a mental health professional who specializes in interviewing children in cases of suspected sexual abuse. This is important for a number of reasons:

1) In a forensic interview, the child is interviewed by a professional in an appropriate, and hopefully legally sound manner. The forensic interviewer is trained to ask non-leading questions that encourage the child to share his experience in his own words.

2) The videotaped interview can be used as evidence in a criminal case and presented as evidence in court.

3) The interview being videotaped should help prevent the child from having to be interviewed about the abuse repeatedly. It may also be possible for the videotape to be presented in court in lieu of the child having to testify, should the case go to court.

4) Children often forget the details of the abuse over time, so it is important for their statements to be recorded as soon as possible after their initial outcry.

Forensic interviews are often arranged through Child Protective Services (CPS) or law enforcement. These agencies may conduct the forensic interviews at their facilities or they may refer the child to a child advocacy center (CAC) to be interviewed. CACs offer coordinated support and services to sexual abuse victims. For a state-by-state listing of accredited CACs, go to the National Children's Alliance website at www.nationalchildrensalliance.org.

It is best to follow the recommendations of CPS and law enforcement and to take your child for the forensic interview scheduled through those agencies. However, there may be some cases when these agencies do not arrange for a forensic interview, such as if the child is very young, the child has not made a clear disclosure, there is no local child advocacy center, or the allegations have surfaced during a custody case. In those cases, you may need to find your own forensic interviewer. You can call 1-800-CHILDREN or go to www.preventchildabuse.org to find your local chapter which should be able to refer you to a forensic interviewer and/or local mental health professional who specializes in cases of alleged sexual abuse.

After the forensic interview has been completed, your child may need to receive counseling to help him or her process his or her thoughts and feelings about the abuse. We will discuss this later in this chapter.

How Children Disclose Sexual Abuse

Children often do not disclose sexual abuse immediately after the abuse occurs, and some children never tell about being sexually abused. For most people, this may not make sense, as they assume that children would tell if they were being abused as they would want the abuse to stop. However, children are often afraid to tell about the abuse, for fear that they will get in trouble for allowing the abuse to occur and for fear that the abuser may hurt them or their loved ones. They may also worry about being separated from their family and being placed in foster care. In some cases, abusers tell the child that if the child tells about the abuse, it will tear the family apart. Children may also not disclose abuse because they are embarrassed to tell about it. In one study, 57% of children with an STD did not tell how they contracted the STD when asked in an interview. Also, children often do not disclose abuse when their parent(s) are not supportive of their allegations. In the STD study, 83% of the children of unsupportive parents failed to disclose their sexual abuse.[1] Thus, if you want your child to disclose any abuse he experiences, it is important to let him know that he should tell you about any such abuse, and that you will believe him. Consider the case of Jessica:

Jessica is a 12-year-old girl in therapy for sexual abuse. When Jessica was 10, her mother began dating a man who eventually moved in with them. Jessica's mother had been struggling to make ends meet, and she frequently referred to this man as their "lifesaver." After the man had been living with them for several months, he went into Jessica's room one night and molested her. He warned her that if she told no one would believe her. Jessica wanted to tell her mother right away, but was afraid that the man would be right, and her mother would not believe her. She also felt conflicted, because the man was providing for them financially. The man sexually abused her several more times. Jessica kept hoping that her mother would break up with him. When Jessica's mother told her that she planned to marry this man, Jessica became upset and told her mother what the man had been doing. Jessica's mother became very angry, accusing Jessica of making up lies to keep her from getting married again. She told Jessica that if it had really happened she would not have waited to tell. Jessica's mother later caught the man in the act, and felt devastated that she had not believed her daughter in the first place. It was not until she got Jessica into treatment that she learned why children sometimes do not tell about sexual abuse right away. She came to understand why her daughter had been reluctant to tell her, and she resolved to improve their communication with each other.

Children often initially deny the abuse when questioned, but later admit that the abuse did occur. In one study, 79% of sexually abused children in confirmed sexual abuse cases initially denied the abuse or were tentative in disclosing it. However, 96% of those children eventually made a clear disclosure over time. Once children disclose sexual abuse, they often offer more information about the abuse over time. In other words, they tend to disclose the abuse slowly, in bits, over time. They may not disclose the information all at once because it is overwhelming to them, it is difficult to talk about, and/or they are testing the water to see how others will respond to their initial disclosure.[2]

Children may minimize the extent of the sexual abuse by underreporting how frequently the sexual abuse occurred or the severity of the sexual acts. For example, in a case of an offender who molested 18 children, the children recounted less than 80% of the sexual activities reported by the offender who had confessed.[3] Children may minimize the extent of the abuse for a variety of reasons. For example, they may feel embarrassed and/or guilty about certain sexual acts or they may have used certain coping strategies during the abuse that helped them "block out" the abuse, which make it difficult to later remember all of the details of the abuse. Children may also not disclose the full extent of the abuse simply because they were never asked specific questions about the abuse. For example, a child may disclose that her uncle touched her "tee tee" but may not think to tell that he also licked her "tee tee" unless specifically asked. Children may also not disclose all of the details of their abuse if they do not feel comfortable with the person who is asking them. Just like adults, children tend to "open up" more with people they feel comfortable with. For example, sexually abused girls may be less likely to openly share their abuse with a male forensic interviewer if they were molested by a male and do not trust males.

Girls are more likely than boys to tell if they have been sexually abused. This may be due to boys often feeling shame and embarrassment about being molested by a male. School-aged children often make their disclosures of abuse to a caregiver while young children are more likely to disclose their abuse accidentally. Preschool age children in particular are most likely to disclose abuse accidentally, as they may not realize that the touching constituted sexual abuse. For example, a 5-year-old boy may comment to his mother that his "wee wee" gets big when his grandfather licks it. The boy may have no idea that he just disclosed sexual abuse. Children also often disclose sexual abuse after they have been caught acting out sexually. For example, 4-year-old Amanda was seen humping other children during naptime in daycare. When asked what she was doing, she said her big brother likes to hump her. Even teenagers sometimes disclose sexual abuse for the first time when they are questioned about their own sexual acting out.

Why Do Children Sometimes Recant their Allegations?

Children sometimes recant or take back their allegations of sexual abuse. On its face, it seems like this means that the abuse did not occur. However, children often recant their allegations even when the abuse did occur. In fact, 22% of children in confirmed cases of sexual abuse recanted their allegations. 92% of those children then reaffirmed their allegations over time[4]. So, the question is why did the children recant in the first place? There can be many different reasons why children recant. For example, a child may recant his or her allegations because:

- The child is afraid of all of the sudden unwanted attention such as being interviewed by the police, having a physical exam, and having to go to court.

- The child starts to realize the negative consequences that can follow a disclosure such as being placed in foster care or the abuser going to jail.

- The abuser or the child's family has pressured them to recant their allegations.

- The child's parent or primary caretaker does not believe the abuse occurred.

- The child is afraid the abuser may harm her family.

- The child wants to return home, if she was placed in foster care as a result of the allegations.

- The child feels guilty because the allegations may have resulted in the abuser having to leave the home, thereby negatively impacting the family. For example, a child may feel guilty if her allegations against the stepfather resulted in the stepfather having to leave the home and the mother being left without a source of income.

- The child does not want to the abuser to go to jail or be punished. This is often the case when the abuser is a family member or loved one.

- The child is afraid of talking to the police or testifying in court.

- The child is tired of being questioned about the abuse and wants to pretend that the abuse never happened.

Rates of False Allegations

Since there have been a number of highly publicized cases about false allegations, people sometimes assume that it is common for children to lie about sexual abuse. However, the research shows that this is not the case. In fact, the rates of false allegations are very low, ranging from 2 to 8% across studies[5]. Thus, it appears to be relatively rare for a child to intentionally lie about sexual abuse. This is consistent with our clinical experience as well. It is more likely for a teenager to lie about sexual abuse than a young child, but false allegations are still relatively rare among teens. As you might expect, adults are 3 times more likely to make false allegations than children[6].

The term "false allegations" refers to allegations that have been shown to be false. This is different from cases that are not substantiated, meaning that there was not enough evidence to determine if the abuse occurred. A much larger percentage of cases, between 50 to 65% are considered unsubstantiated.[7] This is because there is often no hard proof that the abuse occurred, such as no physical evidence, medical evidence, or witnesses.

Physical Evidence of Sexual Abuse

Many people assume that there will be physical evidence in cases of sexual abuse, and that a physical exam can prove whether or not a child has been molested. However, it is rare for there to be physical evidence of sexual abuse. In fact, 95% of sexually abused children have normal genital exams, meaning they showed no physical signs of sexual abuse. There can be many reasons why there is no physical evidence of sexual abuse. It may be because the abuse did not cause any physical damage, as it involved only fondling or oral sex. However, even in proven cases of penetration, up to 95% of the children had normal genital exams.[8]

Time is an important factor in sexual abuse cases, as no physical evidence may be found if the physical exam is done more than 48 hours after the abuse. The child may have showered since the abuse, washing away any evidence of semen or blood. Also, any injuries from the abuse may heal, as young children tend to heal very quickly.

Treatment for the Sexually Abused Child

As we discussed earlier, not all children respond to sexual abuse the same way. There is a wide range of responses to abuse, with some children showing few problems in response to abuse while others show many emotional, behavioral, and/or sexual problems[9]. Given this, we recommend that sexually abused children receive a sexual trauma evaluation, a specialized type of psychological evaluation, to assess how they have been affected by the abuse. This evaluation can then be used to identify which areas should be addressed in treatment. For example, an evaluation may find that a sexually abused boy secretly worries that his molestation by a male means that he is gay. His therapist would then address that concern in his treatment. In another case, an evaluation may find that a child has developed Posttraumatic Stress Disorder in response to the abuse. Treatment would then focus on treating the symptoms of posttraumatic stress. Evaluations can also help determine if your child's symptoms, such as depression or anxiety, are severe enough that your child may benefit from medication to treat the symptoms.

Some children may appear to have no symptoms initially, but may develop symptoms over time. Also, some children who show no symptoms may actually have secret worries or distress that others do not see. For example, they may secretly worry that the abuse is their fault or that others will love them only if they engage in sexual activity. Other children may secretly cut their bodies with razors or other sharp objects as a way to cope with emotional pain. They may hide the cuts so others are not aware of their self-injurious behavior. The point here is that we should not assume that a child is not experiencing distress just because they show no outward symptoms. Sexually abused children may also experience problems later on as they go through adolescence and are faced with puberty and sexual feelings. Thus, sexual trauma evaluations can be helpful, even well after the abuse, to assess the more long-term effects of sexual abuse and the child's evolving treatment needs.

Tasha is a 17-year-old girl. When Tasha was 3, her Uncle James – a favorite relative in the family – began molesting her when she would go stay at his house. James told Tasha that the sexual abuse was a "special" kind of love, and that no one else could know about it. As the years went on and the sexual abuse continued, Tasha began to feel more and more conflicted about what Uncle James was doing to her. Tasha had always been a rather withdrawn child, and told no one of the sexual abuse. As Tasha entered puberty, she developed an eating disorder that involved eating excessive amounts of food and forcing herself to vomit. This seemed to give her a sense of control in at least one area of her life while she felt she had no control over the abuse. She also began cutting on her legs with a razor blade, as she felt emotionally numb and wanted to feel something, even if that was pain.

After Tasha began to develop sexually, Uncle James lost interest in her. While on one hand she was grateful that the abuse stopped, she also felt lonely. She believed that her relationship with Uncle James was the closest she had with anyone. Tasha began going out with various older boys in her school, trying to recapture the distorted "closeness" she had with her uncle. Tasha soon developed a reputation as being promiscuous. At the age of 14 she contracted a sexually transmitted disease. Her mother, still in the dark about the sexual abuse, was perplexed by Tasha's behavior. She put Tasha on birth control and educated her about protecting herself, but continued to fear for Tasha's safety. When Tasha was 16, she ran away from home to stay with a 30-year-old man she had met online. Because Tasha was at the legal age of consent, the man could not be prosecuted for having sex with her. By this time, Uncle James had been arrested for molesting another girl. Tasha's mother asked her about James, and Tasha angrily confirmed that he had molested her for years. By the time Tasha got into treatment, she had developed a number of serious emotional and behavioral problems. Her sexual trauma evaluation identified her eating disorder (Bulimia), cutting behaviors, and distorted beliefs about sex and sexual relationships as major targets for intervention.

Types of Treatment

One of the most effective treatments for sexually abused children is called Trauma Focused Cognitive Behavioral Therapy (TF-CBT). This is a well-researched, short-term therapy that can work in as few as 12 sessions, but can extend longer depending on the child's and the parents' needs[10]. The treatment involves the child and parent each attending individual sessions, as well as joint sessions with both the child and parent.

In TF-CBT, the children and parents learn about the impact of sexual abuse and common reactions to abuse. The parent is taught parenting skills to help the child's emotional and behavioral adjustment, and the child and parent are taught relaxation and stress management skills. In addition, the child and parent are taught healthy ways of expressing and managing emotions. They are also taught about the relationship between thoughts, feelings and behaviors. This can help the child and parent change any inaccurate or unhelpful thoughts about the sexual abuse. The child then begins to tell about their sexual abuse in a process called trauma narration. The child learns strategies to overcome their avoidance of situations that may remind them of their sexual abuse, but are no longer dangerous. The child and parent then have joint sessions to help them talk to each other about the sexual abuse. The final phase of treatment focuses on strategies to increase the child's future safety.

Research shows that TF-CBT reduces symptoms of PTSD, as well as results in improvements in depression, anxiety, behavior problems, sexualized behaviors, trauma-related shame, trust in others, and social competence. For more information about how this type of therapy can help your child, see the National Child Trauma Stress Network's video called *The Promise of Trauma-Focused Treatment for Child Sexual Abuse* at www.nctsn.org.

Counselors may also use other treatment techniques including yoga to help children learn to relax, self-soothe, and feel reconnected to their bodies. In addition, some counselors may use supportive therapy or play therapy to help children express their thoughts and feelings about the abuse. The general idea is that treatment provides the child with an opportunity to process their thoughts and feelings about the abuse, to correct any distorted beliefs the child may have about the abuse, and to address any symptoms or problems the child has developed in response to the abuse. The good news is that with the right kind of counseling, sexually abused children can recover completely and go on to lead normal, happy lives.

There are many different resources available to help you find a therapist who specializes in treating sexual abuse:

- The National Child Traumatic Stress Network's *Finding Help* page at http://www.nctsn.org/nccts/nav.do?pid=ctr_gethelp

- Prevent Child Abuse at 1-800-CHILDREN or go to www.preventchildabuse.org

- American Psychological Association Therapist Locator page at http://locator.apa.org/

- American Association for Marriage and Family Therapy's Therapist Locator page: http://www.therapistlocator.net

How Your Child's Disclosure Affects You

It is normal to feel very upset when your child discloses sexual abuse. Parents may feel shocked, depressed, helpless, confused, angry, and/or unsure what to do next. It may be particularly painful if you experienced sexual abuse yourself as a child, as your child's disclosure may bring up old memories and unresolved feelings. If this is the case, we recommend that you get help and support for yourself as this can help both you and your child cope with the situation. You can contact the Rape, Abuse, and Incest National Network (RAINN) at 1-800-656-HOPE or go to www.rainn.org for help finding support in your area. You can also go to the website for the U.S. Department of Justice's Office for Victims of Crime at http://www.ojp.usdoj.gov/ovc/ for resources and a web forum to communicate with others about topics related to child abuse, court preparation, and victim's rights.

In addition to being upset, some parents may have difficulty believing their child is telling the truth. They may look for ways to discount and dismiss the child's account because it is too painful and upsetting to believe that the abuse has occurred, particularly if the abuser is a loved one or family member. We have seen many cases like this where the parents discounted their child's allegations and took no further action. As a result, the children were often molested again and/or the abuser went on to molest others. The victim was also often left feeling unsupported and emotionally abandoned, which can lead to significant anger, resentment, depression, and acting out. Given this, we strongly encourage you to follow up with a mental health professional any time your child makes an outcry of sexual abuse or makes statements that could be suggestive of sexual abuse. By doing this, you will know that you have done the right thing by taking steps to find out if your child has been abused.

When Sexual Abuse Occurs Within the Family

When sexual abuse is discovered in the home, the abuser is often required by Child Protective Services or law enforcement to leave the home. This is generally recommended, particularly for abusers who are teens or adults. Families can be reunified after sexual abuse has occurred in the family, assuming that the sexual abuse is adequately addressed in counseling and assuming that reunification is in the abused child's emotional best interest.

Reunification is not recommended in cases where the abuser, victim, and/or the family:

- deny the abuse occurred
- refuse to address the sexual abuse in treatment
- are not willing to follow a safety plan to ensure the victim is never left alone with the abuser

Reunification is also not recommended if the abuser's risk for reoffending is too high for him or her to live in the same home with his victim. In addition, reunification is not recommended if the victim feels unsafe living with the abuser.

Ideally, before reunification is considered, the following should occur:

1) The victim should receive individual counseling to help her process her thoughts and feelings about the sexual abuse;
2) The abuser should attend and complete a sex offender treatment program;
3) The family should receive family therapy to address the sexual abuse and the family dynamics that may have

contributed to the abuse; and

4) The victim and abuser have a "clarification" therapy session together in which the abuser apologizes to his victim, takes full responsibility for his behavior, and the victim has the chance to ask the abuser questions.

Assuming all of these steps go well, the victim then typically begins having short supervised visits with the abuser. If these supervised visits go well, the visits become more frequent and longer, progressing to overnight visits. It is very important that the family follow a safety plan to ensure that the victim is supervised at all times around the abuser, to decrease the risk of the abuse occurring again. Assuming the overnight visits go well, the visits may expand to weekend visits and eventually result in the abuser moving back into the home with the victim. However, it is recommended that both the victim and abuser continue to attend counseling for at least several months after the reunification, to ensure that the reunification process is going smoothly. Specifically, ongoing counseling can assess if the victim feels safe, the safety plan is being followed, and the abuser is able to successfully manage his high-risk thoughts and feelings that could lead to reoffense.

There is no set timeline for the reunification process, as it depends on how the victim, abuser, and family respond to treatment. However, sex offender treatment of teens or adults typically takes a year or more. Thus, reunification is typically not recommended for at least a year in those cases. Families often want to rush the reunification process, as they are eager for their families to reunite. However, rushing the process is not recommended, especially since it places pressure on the victim and can result in premature reunification and the abuser reoffending.

Conclusion

Having your child tell you they have been sexually abused is one of the most distressing things that can happen to a parent. If such a thing does happen, it is important to remember that you are *not* helpless. Your response can go a long way to protect your child and help their recovery.

---

[1] Lawson, L., & Chaffin, M. (1992). False negatives in sexual abuse disclosure interviews: Incidence and influence of caretaker's belief in abuse in cases of accidental abuse discovery by diagnosis of STD, *Journal of Interpersonal Violence*, 7, 532-542.

[2] Sorensen, T., & Snow, B. (1991), How children tell: The process of disclosure in child sexual abuse. *Child Welfare*,70, 3-15.

[3] Terry, W. (1991). Perpetrator and victim accounts of sexual abuse. Paper presented at the Conference on the Health Science Response to Child Maltreatment, San Diego, CA.

[4] Sorensen, T., & Snow, B. (1991), How children tell: The process of disclosure in child sexual abuse. *Child Welfare*,70, 3-15.

[5] Everson, M., & Boat, B. (1989), False Allegations of Sexual Abuse by Children and Adolescents, *Journal of the American Academy of Child and Adolescent Psychiatry*, 2:230-235.

[6] Jones, D., & McGraw, E. (1987), Reliable and fictitious accounts of sexual abuse to children. *Journal of Interpersonal Violence*, 2(1), 27-45.,

[7] American Association for Protecting Children, 1988

[8] Heger, A., Ticson, L., Velasquez, O., & Bernier, R. (2002). Children referred for possible sexual abuse: medical findings in 2384 children. *Child Abuse & Neglect*, 26, 645-59.

[9] Briere, J. & Elliott, D.M. (1994), Immediate and Long-Term Impacts of Sexual Abuse, *Sexual Abuse of Children*, Vol 4, No. 2

[10] How to Implement Trauma-Focused Cognitive Behavioral Therapy, National Child Traumatic Stress Network Child Sexual Abuse Task Force, 2.

[10] Lawson, L., & Chaffin, M. (1992). False negatives in sexual abuse disclosure interviews: Incidence and influence of caretaker's belief in abuse in cases of accidental abuse discovery by diagnosis of STD, *Journal of Interpersonal Violence,* 7, 532-542.

[10] Sorensen, T., & Snow, B. (1991), How children tell: The process of disclosure in child sexual abuse. *Child Welfare,* 70, 3-15.

[10] Terry, W. (1991). Perpetrator and victim accounts of sexual abuse. Paper presented at the Conference on the Health Science Response to Child Maltreatment, San Diego, CA.

[10] Sorensen, T., & Snow, B. (1991), How children tell: The process of disclosure in child sexual abuse. *Child Welfare,*70, 3-15.

[10] Everson, M., & Boat, B. (1989), False Allegations of Sexual Abuse by Children and Adolescents, *Journal of the American Academy of Child and Adolescent Psychiatry,* 2:230-235.

Appendix: Setting Parental Controls on Your Computer

Chapter 7 discusses various blocking programs (such as NetNanny) that help block access to inappropriate programs. However, your computer already has useful parental controls built in to the operating system. For a computing novice, setting the parental controls on your computer can be a daunting prospect. This appendix will give you step-by-step instructions for doing so.

If you have Windows Vista

1. Click on the Windows logo in the bottom left-hand corner of the screen.
2. A little screen will pop up that has a list of terms running down the right-hand side. Click on "Control Panel." It's close to the bottom.
3. Now a window comes up with many icons. Scroll down to the one that says "Parental Controls" and double-click on it.
4. The computer will now give you a list of user accounts to select from.
   a. If you already have created an account for your child, click on it. Note that Vista will not allow you to put parental controls on a user account that has "administrator" privileges (see chapter 7 for more information about what this means). So your child's account must be what is called "limited access."
   b. If you have *not* already created an account for your child, Vista will now allow you to do so.

5. Once the account has been selected, you are taken to a window that says "Set up how [account name] will use the computer." This window has many options for parents. They can choose what times their child is able to use the computer – so, for example, they can prevent their child from using the computer when the parent is at work. Parents can also choose how much access to give their child to the Internet, which games to allow their child to use, and they can block access to specific programs. This window also has the option to gather information on what the child is doing on the account, including what websites they have been visiting. On the right-hand side of the screen is an option labeled "View Activity Reports," which will give the parent an overview of what their child has been doing on the computer.

If you have Windows 7

The setup for Windows 7 is very similar to that for Windows Vista. However, Windows 7 does *not* have the options of website filtering or providing reports on your child's activity. To enable these options you must download and install additional software. Microsoft offers a package through Windows Live called "Windows Live Family Safety." Other options include such third-party providers as NetNanny.

If you have a Macintosh Computer (running the "Leopard" or "Snow Leopard" operating systems)

1. Click on "System Preferences" – it's the icon that looks like a gear, and it should be one of the icons that runs along the bottom of the screen (called the "dock").
2. Click on "Parental Controls" – the icon is a yellow circle that has stick figures of an adult and child inside it.
3. The window that comes up asks you to select a user account so you can adjust the parent controls. This should be an account created for your child. You will

probably be asked to click on a little lock icon at the bottom left-hand of the screen, which will prompt you to enter your password (the one you set up when you first got the computer).

4. Once you've entered your password, you will be given a number of options:
    a. The "Apps" option allows you to limit the programs your child can use on the computer.
    b. The "Web" option allows you to control what websites your child can access.
    c. The "People" option allows you to select who your child can communicate with online – either through email or the computer's built-in webcam.
    d. The "Time Limits" option allow you to limit the amount of time your child can spend on the computer, and also block access during selected hours (such as nighttime).
    e. The "Other" option provides miscellaneous choices for the parent, including limiting access to the printer, preventing CD or DVD burning, or preventing the child from changing their own password.

About the Authors

Dr. Medlin is a psychologist who has expertise in evaluating and treating sex offenders and sexual abuse victims. Dr. Medlin obtained her bachelor's degree in psychology from Harvard University, and her master's and doctoral degrees in Clinical Psychology from the University of Florida. Dr. Medlin serves as the Director of the Medlin Training Institute (MTI), which specializes in training other professionals in the area of sexual abuse and sexual deviancy. Dr. Medlin published *Responsible Living,* a sex offender treatment manual, along with a CD-ROM entitled *Breaking Through Denial*. Dr. Medlin has provided numerous trainings for mental health professionals and correctional staff. Dr. Medlin has testified as an expert in court over 150 times, and has served as the sex offender treatment consultant to the Probation Division of the Georgia Department of Corrections. Dr. Medlin is Past President of the Georgia Association for the Treatment of Sexual Abusers. She also served on the Georgia Child Sexual Abuse Prevention Advisory Council and on the Georgia Sex Offender Registration Review Board. In addition, Dr. Medlin has appeared as an expert on national televisions programs for CNN and Discovery Health, as well as several nationally syndicated programs.

Dr. Knauts is a clinical psychologist who specializes in assessing and treating sexual issues in children, adolescents, and adults. Dr. Knauts graduated from the University of Utah magna cum laude with a BA in Psychology. He received his M.S. and Ph.D. in Clinical Psychology from the University of Florida. Dr. Knauts has done clinical work at several forensic facilities, including North Florida Evaluation and Treatment Center and Florida State Hospital. In addition to *Avoiding Sexual Dangers*, Dr. Knauts co-authored a CD-ROM called *Breaking Through Denial*. He has provided group and individual therapy for adolescents and adults with sexual problems, and has provided individual therapy for children with sexual and/or behavioral problems. Dr. Knauts has conducted psychological, psychosexual, and parenting evaluations, and has testified as an expert witness on numerous occasions. Dr. Knauts has conducted trainings for other mental health professionals, foster parents, and the community. He has given presentations for such organizations as Prevent Child Abuse Georgia, Georgia CASA, the Georgia Association for the Treatment of Sexual Abusers, and the National Organization for Victim Assistance.